PUFFIN BOOKS
A BAGFUL OF HISTORY

Subhadra Sen Gupta has written over forty books for children because she thinks they are the best readers in the world. She writes on history; imagines mystery, ghost and adventure stories; and dreams up comic books. She is waiting for one of her young readers to build a time machine so that she can exchange some funny stories with Birbal and then join Emperor Akbar for a royal lunch.

If you have any questions, complaints, crazy ideas or comments, write to her at subhadrasg@gmail.com.

ALSO IN PUFFIN BY SUBHADRA SEN GUPTA

A BAGFUL OF HISTORY

SUBHADRA SEN GUPTA

Illustrations by Tapas Guha

PUFFIN BOOKS

An imprint of Penguin Random House

PUFFIN BOOKS

USA | Canada | UK | Ireland | Australia
New Zealand | India | South Africa | China | Singapore

Puffin Books is part of the Penguin Random House group of companies
whose addresses can be found at global.penguinrandomhouse.com

Published by Penguin Random House India Pvt. Ltd
4th Floor, Capital Tower 1, MG Road,
Gurugram 122 002, Haryana, India

Penguin
Random House
India

First published in Puffin Books by Penguin Random House India 2018

ISBN 9780143442240

Typeset in Archer by Manipal Digital Systems, Manipal
Printed at Manipal Technologies Limited, India

www.penguin.co.in

MIX
Paper | Supporting
responsible forestry
FSC® C043100
FSC
www.fsc.org

This is a legitimate digitally printed version of the book and therefore might not
have certain extra finishing on the cover.

For Tapas Guha,
who has made my stories come alive with
his illustrations, which capture the essence of
a tale with a few strokes of his pencil.
With love and a big thank you.

CONTENTS

PREFACE

In these dozen stories you will travel back in time to the India of the past. But I promise you these stories are much more interesting than your history lessons!

These are stories about how children lived in the times of King Ashoka, Emperor Akbar, Raja Raja Chola and during the Uprising of 1857. You will meet Mughal princesses, a magical drummer and a very bad-tempered Lucknowi nawab. Also, there are gentle Buddhist monks, excited soldiers and a ghost or two.

After you read these stories, you'll agree that history can be pretty interesting—because it is the story of our land and its people. It is not just about deadly dull dates and impossible-to-spell names of kings. And I totally agree with all history students that three kings named Chandragupta is very unfair!

So let us go time-travelling, and I promise you the journey will be great fun!

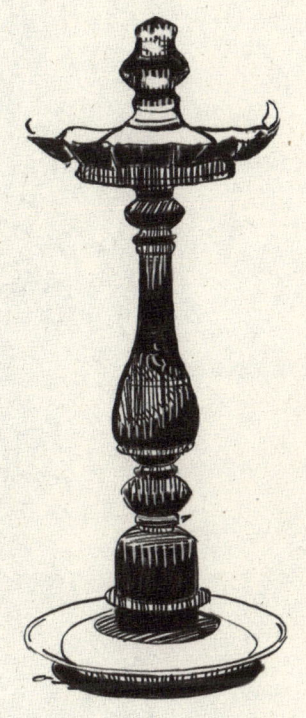

A Long, Long
Time Ago . . .

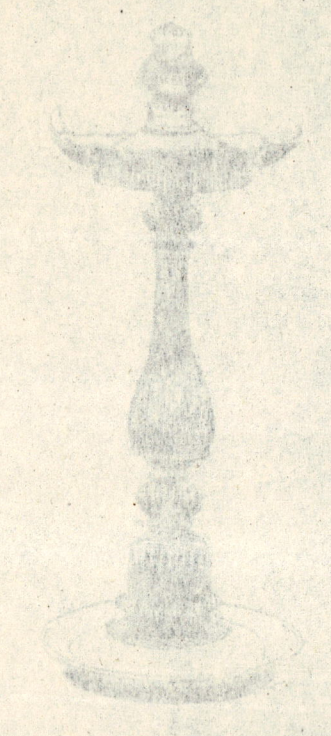

The Young Monk

The bullock cart rolled to a halt at the gate of the Buddhist vihara.

'Why are the gates of the monastery closed?' Laxman looked puzzled as he pulled at the reins of the bullock to make it stop.

'And who's that?' Parvati pointed to a man standing grimly at the gate. He wore the uniform of a soldier— a sleeveless leather vest over his long-sleeved jacket, pyjamas and a tall turban. He was carrying a spear and had a sword hanging from a leather belt around his waist.

Nakul looked surprised. 'What's a soldier doing at the Pataliputra vihara? Guarding what? This is a monastery!'

The soldier stared back stonily but did not move to open the gate. So the children climbed down from the cart and went to him.

'Sir, can we go in, please?' Laxman asked politely.

A round-cheeked, moustached face was lowered threateningly. 'I have no orders to open the gate for bullock carts.'

'But, sir,' Parvati waved towards the cart that was piled high with pottery—lamps, plates, bowls—'we have brought the pottery that was ordered by Bhikshu Aditya from my father's pottery shop.'

At Bhikshu Aditya's name the man stiffened, then muttered, 'Wait here . . .' and marched off inside. He came back shortly and swung open the gate. 'You can come in, but go out by the back gate when you leave.'

'Yes, sir!' Laxman nodded before they clambered back on to the cart and entered the vihara. 'Back gate it will be. We potters can't use the main gate, can we?' he muttered angrily under his breath. 'That's for the chariots of the rich!'

Parvati and Nakul laughed. If the soldier heard Laxman, it did not show on his stiff, expressionless face.

Laxman and his younger sister, Parvati, were the children of one of the best potters in the city of Pataliputra. Everyone needed pottery for their homes, especially their kitchens, and so the potters, like the weavers, were the richest among the city's craftsmen. Their childhood friend Nakul was the son of a soldier. His father was often away guarding the borders of the kingdom of Magadha, so he spent most of his time

4

with them, even learning to use the potter's wheel along with Laxman.

Parvati and her mother collected clay from the banks of the Ganga River, clearing it of stones and kneading it until it became soft and pliable like dough. From this Parvati's father made the cooking and water pots, bowls, lamps and plates on his potter's wheel. Then the pottery was fired in a kiln, after which they painted pretty patterns on it using the white of lime powder and lampblack. Thus was made the special black ware pottery of Pataliputra that was famous across the world, with shiploads being taken to other countries by merchants.

It was Parvati who had first met the monk Bhikshu Aditya. One morning she had been working in the courtyard, trimming the jasmine bush, when she'd heard the clang of a bell at the gate. She turned to see a monk standing there. He had a shaven head, was barefoot and clad in saffron robes, and he carried a walking stick and a begging bowl. Parvati called out, 'Wait, please, Bhikshu!' making the monk smile as she ran inside to get a bowl of rice, lentils and vegetables.

These monks were Buddhist and so Parvati knew that they went out begging for food in the morning and that at noon they cooked and ate their sole meal of the day. Aditya later told the children that begging taught the monks humility and simplicity, and that even their great teacher, Gautama Buddha, would beg for alms every morning. The monks spent the rest of the day working around the vihara, praying, meditating and reading sacred books.

Soon Aditya had become their friend, and they would often meet him at the vihara, where he started teaching them to read and write. Before long, Laxman was keeping all the accounts of the pottery business, and he was even better at it than his father.

His father had once told Aditya, 'Even I'd wanted to learn to read, write and count, Bhikshu, but when I was a boy, we only had Brahmin teachers in our locality. I'd gone to the priest at the temple but he'd laughed at me, saying no son of a potter could be educated. We belong to a low caste after all.'

'The Buddha said that there is nothing called caste. It is a thing created by Brahmins. We are born equal and we all have a right to be educated,' replied the monk.

'I too was amazed to hear the Buddha's teachings and that is why when a vihara opened nearby, we all went and joined the Buddhist sangha,' Laxman had said.

Soon Aditya became the head of the vihara, and he began to order pottery from their shop. So, in addition to their lessons, the children often went to the monastery to deliver cartloads of earthenware. It was the main vihara in Pataliputra, where even King Ashoka and his family came to worship. Of course, that did not mean Bhikshu Aditya stopped begging for food. Many a time he would arrive at their gate, smiling and clanging his begging bowl, and Parvati would run up with rice, vegetables and fruit.

The children rode to the back of the monastery, where the kitchens and storerooms were located. As the cart drew up to the pottery store, an unfamiliar young monk came out and said with a smile, 'Oh, good! The pottery is here.' Then, as the children began unloading the pots and dishes, he came forward, saying, 'Oh, let me help you . . .'

'Carry them carefully, Bhikshu,' Laxman warned. 'If anything breaks, my baba will kill me!'

The young monk flashed an amused smile. 'Don't worry. I'll be very, *very* careful.'

Once the wares were stacked up on shelves, the young monk looked closely at two lamps covered with intricate patterns in black and white. 'This is beautiful! Who's the artist in your family?'

Parvati grinned. 'Amma and I. I make up the designs as I draw them.'

After checking that all the pottery had been delivered, the young monk hurried off to the vihara office. He came back with a handful of silver *pana* and copper *karshapana* coins, which he gave to Laxman.

Always the careful businessman, Laxman carefully counted the money, put the coins into a cloth bag tied to his waist and tucked it inside his dhoti. At this the young monk laughed softly.

As the three were climbing on to the cart, which Nakul offered to ride, the young monk asked suddenly, 'Where will you go now?'

'Our home in the potters' lane.'

'May I come with you? It's *such* a long walk to the city, and it's so hot!' Then the young monk shrugged, adding, 'Though I have no money to give you.'

Laxman laughed. 'We know that *bhikshus* never carry any money. Where do you have to go?'

The young monk hesitated for a moment and then said, 'Near the palace.'

'No problem!' Nakul picked up the reins. 'We'll go past the palace. Come on up!'

With Laxman, Parvati and the young monk settled on the empty cart, Nakul pulled at the reins and clicked his tongue to tell the bullock to start moving.

'Through the back gate,' Laxman reminded Nakul.

'I remember,' Nakul muttered.

'Why have they closed the main gate?' Parvati asked the young monk. 'They've put a soldier there and he wouldn't let us in.'

'Oh really?' The young monk looked surprised. 'I have no idea! But I do know that the back gate is open, so we can go through there.'

'You *should* know about the soldier. You live here.'

'Well . . . actually . . .' He gave an apologetic shrug. 'I only came here last week. I was studying in Takshashila for many years before that.' Wiping the sweat off his brow with the edge of his robe, he said, 'It's so much cooler there.'

Peacefully they rolled along the road towards the city of Pataliputra, the capital of the kingdom of Magadha, ruled by Ashoka, the great king of the Mauryan dynasty, son of Bindusara and grandson of Chandragupta. The new vihara had been built on the outskirts of the city and they had to enter Pataliputra through high wooden gates, where soldiers checked everyone. There was a towering boundary wall on both sides of the gate, made of thick logs of wood, and more soldiers stood on top. It was said that Pataliputra never slept. All day and all night long, the city was busy with people, the markets buzzing with trade, and at night the gates were shut so that no one could enter or leave. Even then, torches were lit on top of the gates and the soldiers marched around.

The cart entered a busy street and joined the daily bustle of one of the greatest cities of the kingdom. Near the river the fisherwomen had spread out the day's catch, the rows of fish gleaming silver in the sun. Next to them sat the vegetable and fruit sellers with piles of green spinach, many kinds of gourds, peas, bananas and pears. Laxman spotted mangoes and, as he had the money, hopped off the cart to buy some. He remarked that mangoes made the summer heat worth it, and the monk laughed and agreed. Then they entered a market where the shops were just opening their doors to sell textiles, jewellery, woodcraft and pottery. And at the food shops the *chullah*s were being lit, the smoke floating across the road. The air was full of the calls of shopkeepers seeking customers.

'The best baskets in the city!'

'Come and see my copper pots!'

'Cloth from Kalinga! Silks from Kashi!'

The young monk was looking around with a smile, his eyes shining with happiness. 'Oh, I had forgotten about the markets. There's the flower seller, and that lady makes such wonderful paan . . .'

'You used to live here?' Parvati asked curiously.

'Well, I was born in Ujjaini and then we came here—' He paused as if he had said too much. 'I grew up in Pataliputra and later went to Takshashila to study.'

'Your father must be very rich,' Nakul commented, 'to be able to send you so far away.'

The young monk paused, as if he had to think about it, and then said casually, 'He works in the government and we have some land too.'

'And now you've become a monk! Wasn't he disappointed?' Laxman asked. 'Didn't he want you to become an officer, or a soldier?'

The young monk shook his head. 'My father knew from the time I was about fifteen that I wanted to join the sangha. So I went to the vihara in Takshashila to study the sacred texts.'

'We are followers of Sakyamuni too.' Parvati smiled at him. Perched in the back of the cart, she was the first to notice the man in the green turban. She vaguely remembered him walking behind their cart as they'd left the vihara through the back gate. And now here he was, still strolling behind the cart half an hour later! She'd spotted him because she had a skirt in exactly that shade of green. The man had tied one end of the turban around his mouth, against the rising dust, and so all she could see were his huge dark eyes under narrow, curving brows.

As they neared the king's palace, the traffic became louder and more crowded—horse-drawn chariots, bullock carts, handcarts, pedestrians, men riding horses and even an occasional elephant could be seen. The riders were yelling as chariots and carts got stuck, and some even began to fight as the clouds of dust made their eyes sting.

'Oh, I had forgotten this too!' The young monk wiped the dust and the sweat off his face. 'The air in Takshashila is so clean and cool, and it is much quieter there!'

'So you miss your old vihara?' Nakul wanted to know.

'A little.' He nodded. 'Pataliputra is so loud and confusing, and the people are always pushing and shoving. No one has the time for simple courtesy . . .' Then he said, 'Oh, drop me off there! I can walk the rest of the way,' pointing to the end of the road, where the high brick walls of the palace reared up, with a row of flags at the gates snapping in the breeze. The young monk scrambled down from the cart with a quick thank you and walked down the road. Parvati noticed the man in the green turban hurry past them and follow him.

'Bhaiya,' she said to Laxman, 'see that man in the green turban? He's been walking behind us all the way from the vihara. And now he's following the monk!'

Nakul guided the bullock to the side of the road, where they sat watching the young monk and the man in the green turban. The monk was walking easily towards the palace and then, to their surprise, they saw him go to one of the palace gates and speak to the soldier guarding it. Then the soldier bowed and opened the gate, and the young monk disappeared inside.

'He said he had to go *near the palace—*' Laxman said.

'And here he is going straight inside!' Nakul exclaimed.

'Who is he?' Parvati wondered aloud.

Meanwhile, the man in the green turban stood across the road, also watching the young monk enter the palace. Then the three saw a second man walk out of a side lane and stand beside the turbaned one, and the two began to talk, their heads bent towards each other. Laxman hopped down from the cart and casually strolled past the men—the road was so crowded with pedestrians that the two did not notice a boy hovering behind them for a moment and then walking away very, very slowly.

The men were talking very softly, and Laxman only heard fragments of their conversation.

The man with the green turban had been saying, 'He travelled . . . vihara . . . cart . . . children . . .'

'Where did he . . .'

'There . . . What do I do next?' with a wave towards the palace.

'We have to report . . . Bhairava . . .'

As Laxman climbed back on to the cart, Nakul got the vehicle moving and the three rather puzzled children headed home, their heads bursting with questions.

'Did you notice he never told us his name?'

'He must be important—that soldier at the gate bowed to him.'

'But he wanted us to go through the back gate when we left the vihara.'

Then, as the children watched, the man in the green turban entered one of the lanes and vanished.

The next morning, Parvati was helping her mother in the kitchen, chopping beans and onions, when she heard the clang of Bhikshu Aditya's walking stick against his metal begging bowl. She gathered a bundle of rotis and some cooked vegetables and headed for the gate of their courtyard.

As she went up to Aditya, she noticed that he was not smiling when he asked, 'Parvati, did you, Laxman and Nakul go to the vihara yesterday?'

'Yes, Bhikshu. We delivered the pottery you had ordered.'

Aditya bent an anxious face towards her. 'And did you meet a young monk working in the pottery storeroom?'

'Yes, we did, and he was very kind. He even helped us put the pots and dishes on the shelves!'

'Then what happened?'

'When we were leaving, he asked us for a ride to the city, and he rode back on the cart with us.'

'Oh! And where did you drop him off?'

'Um . . . he said he wanted to get off *near* the palace, but then we saw him enter the palace through one of the smaller gates on the side.'

Immediately Aditya's face cleared with relief. 'You are sure, Parvati, that he went into the palace?'

'Yes, he did, Bhikshu, and the guard at the gate bowed to him too.'

'Oh! Then it's fine!' Aditya smiled for the first time that morning and suddenly reached forward to touch Parvati's head in blessing. 'Thank you, my child, and bless you!'

'But for what?' Parvati asked, puzzled, but by then Aditya had turned and hurried away.

The city had separate lanes for different craftspeople. When you walked through the wood carvers' lane, you heard the banging of hammers and the scraping of chisels. The air was full of the clacking sound of the looms in the weavers' locality, and the potters' lane was often wreathed in smoke when the baking kilns were fired. During the hot summers, all work slowed down in the potters' locality by the afternoon, as then the various tasks—starting with igniting the kilns— began at the crack of dawn, when the air was cool. Then in the cool of the evening, the wheels would begin to whirl again, as muddy hands took a lump of clay and turned it into narrow-necked water jars, broad cooking pots and round bowls. It was like magic.

That afternoon, Parvati and Laxman were sitting on mats on the floor of their veranda, decorating two large water jars that had been ordered by a rich tradesman who liked all his pottery to look pretty. Laxman had cut out narrow patterns, like they were lace, and was shaping two curved handles by pleating these clay strips.

'Bhikshu Aditya came by this morning,' Parvati began, absently moulding a ball of clay into the shape of a cat.

'Mmm . . .' Laxman was busy with his design and not really listening to her.

'He asked a very strange question . . .'

Laxman looked up. *'Strange?'*

So she told him of the puzzling conversation she had had with Aditya.

'And he looked relieved when you said we saw the young monk enter the palace?'

Parvati nodded. 'That's the first time he smiled today, and you know he always looks so calm and happy. Today, he'd been looking anxious.'

'How odd!' Laxman had stopped working on the jar handles. 'I wonder who that young monk is.'

'He must be an important person, Bhaiya, if he can just wander into the palace and have guards bow to him! Remember, whenever Baba has to deliver pottery to the royal kitchen, he has to carry a strip of palm leaf stating the order and even then the guards ask him a dozen questions!'

'And he goes himself—never sends us.'

'True. It's not easy to get into the palace.'

Laxman was frowning when he asked, 'Did you tell him about the turbaned man who was following us?'

Parvati shook her head. 'I never got a chance. The moment Bhikshu Aditya heard that the young monk had entered the palace, he quickly blessed me and rushed off.' Then she brooded before adding, 'Actually . . . I did not even think of Green Turban Man!'

Later, in the evening, as they played marbles on the street, Laxman told Nakul about Aditya's peculiar behaviour.

'I think they must have found the young monk missing from the vihara,' Nakul said, closing one eye and taking careful aim, but missing. 'Perhaps Bhikshu Aditya was relieved to figure out that he had gone to the palace.'

'A monk who visits the palace . . . he *must* be an important person.'

'Then we should tell Bhikshu Aditya about Green Turban Man.'

'I think so too. Let's go to him tomorrow morning.'

The next morning, Laxman, Parvati and Nakul headed for the vihara. They could not take the cart as Laxman's father was using it to deliver pottery. So they hitched a ride on a bullock cart that was delivering vegetables to a market. They sat in the back, their feet dangling, shelling peas and popping them into their mouths.

They hopped off at the street corner and walked to the vihara gate, where the same soldier stood on guard while staring grimly ahead.

'Back gate again!' Laxman muttered as they went around the wall and, to their surprise, they saw that the back gate was also closed.

'What's happening here?' Nakul asked, puzzled. 'The gates are never closed . . . and this is the first time I've seen guards at the back gate.'

'Now how do we get in?' Laxman stood there with his hands on his hips and looking very bad-tempered. He waved at the high brick walls of the vihara, saying, 'There's no way we can climb that wall, but it's important we talk to Bhikshu Aditya.'

Parvati scratched her nose thoughtfully. 'Remember the time we helped Bhikshu Aditya pick mangoes in the orchard at the back?'

'Of course! Why didn't I think of that?' Laxman nodded.

There was a small gate that connected the orchard to the kitchen garden, and as the monks worked there, it was always kept open. The children drifted through the orchard, keeping an eye out for guards, but no one lurked under the shadows of the huge, leafy mango trees. At one end was a low wall with the open gate, and there was no soldier in sight. Walking through the garden, with its rows of carrots, radishes and pumpkins, they saw busy monks digging, planting and weeding, and some smiled at them as they passed by.

It was a very big vihara, and they had no idea where Aditya would be. Rows of tiny rooms, in which the monks lived, ran around a courtyard. They peered into Aditya's room, but it was empty. All that it had was a narrow mattress on the floor, an earthen lamp, a water pot and a small wooden chest that contained his saffron robes.

'They really live like the poor,' Parvati said, looking around. 'Bhikshu Aditya once told me that he owned just two robes.'

'And he is the abbot of the vihara . . .'

They wandered through the courtyard, which was dotted with small stupas—the egg-shaped structures in which the ashes of great monks were buried. The monks often prayed at the stupas, and the children could see incense sticks and bunches of flowers around them. Then the three went past the tailoring rooms, where monks were stitching and repairing robes, their needles flying. Outside the kitchen, one monk sat peeling and chopping vegetables, while some others were bathing in the pond and washing their clothes. The vihara was a busy place, yet it was quiet and very peaceful.

The children spotted two monks with begging bowls heading out, and Parvati said worriedly, 'Oh, I hope Bhikshu Aditya hasn't left on his begging rounds already. Then we'll *never* find him today!'

'Let's check the *chaitya.*'

As they neared the chaitya, they could hear the low hum of the monks reciting mantras and there was a whiff of incense in the air. This was the main prayer hall of the vihara and, peering in, they spotted Aditya sitting before the altar, praying with his eyes closed as his fingers turned his prayer beads. On the altar were lamps and sacred carvings of Gautama Buddha's feet; fragrant incense smoke rose in the air and flowers lay piled around the carvings.

The three sat at the back of the long hall, whose pillars and walls were covered with paintings showing the life of the Buddha, and waited patiently for Aditya to complete his prayers. Finally the monk bent forward, touching his forehead to the floor, and then sat up. Turning, he saw them.

'Oh!' His eyes widened in surprise. 'What are you three doing here so early in the morning?'

'Yesterday,' Parvati began, 'you asked me about that young monk who was working in the pottery storeroom...'

'Who is he, Bhikshu?' Nakul asked.

'Did we do something wrong in offering him a ride to the city?' Laxman asked a little nervously.

'Oh no ... no ...' Aditya waved a dismissive hand in the air. 'It's just that he left without taking my permission and did not return by night. I checked at the palace after talking to Parvati here—he's still there and will be back today.'

'He lives in the palace? Is he a member of the royal family?'

'Many people live in the palace, Laxman.'

'Yes, but we saw a guard bow to him.'

Aditya stood there silently, as if he did not know how to reply to their questions, before deciding to answer their question with another one. 'Why do you want to know all this?'

The children exchanged a quick glance, and then Laxman said, 'We saw something else. A man followed our bullock cart from the vihara to the palace. Parvati saw him first.'

'He kept walking behind us all the way ... and, you know, a cart moves slowly and he would stop when we stopped. Then he stood and watched the young monk enter the palace.'

'What did he look like?'

'I only saw his eyes as he had the end of his turban tied around his face.'

'Then another man came up and they started to talk, and so I walked past them but couldn't hear much. Their voices were very low.'

Aditya was frowning now, and the old anxious look was back in his eyes as he made them sit down again. 'Tell me everything that happened that morning, right from the time you met Mah—er ... the young monk.'

So they described in detail all the events of that morning. Aditya wanted to know what the young monk had talked about with them and also where the man in the green turban had headed from the palace.

Finally, Laxman asked gently, 'That young monk is Prince Mahendra, isn't he? We had heard that the king's oldest son was going to join the sangha.'

Aditya nodded. 'He is still a novice but will soon take his vows as a bhikshu and join our vihara as it is the vihara of the royal family. That is why he has returned to Pataliputra.' He stared at their young, listening faces and added, 'I want you three to promise not to tell anyone about it, please. Not even your family.'

'So *that* is why there are soldiers at the gates!'

'Yes. Any member of the royal family has to be guarded, even though he may be a poor monk.' Aditya sighed and remarked, 'Mahendra is young, and he dislikes all the fuss and does not always obey me. I had told him that he has to take my permission before leaving the vihara, and I would have sent him to the palace in a chariot with an armed soldier if he had—but he hates that. Even in Takshashila he used to wander around and chat with people in the markets and streets.'

'He said that he misses Takshashila.'

'What he doesn't realize is that it is much more dangerous for him in Pataliputra, where there are many enemies of the royal family.'

'So who do you think that man in the green turban was?'

Aditya shrugged. 'I have no idea! I'll have to go to the palace and report all this to the royal ministers.'

'Do you think His Majesty will scold Prince Mahendra?' Parvati asked anxiously.

Aditya laughed as they got up. 'I think Prince Mahendra can handle a little scolding. You three go home now, and thank you so much for your help.'

They looked around as they left the vihara by the back gate, but Green Turban Man was nowhere in sight. But then, as Nakul pointed out, the prince was now safe in the palace.

'I wish I could find out who Green Turban Man is ...' Parvati began.

'He went into a lane opposite the palace, remember?' Nakul said keenly. 'We could check out that lane, couldn't we?'

'And go around asking, "Have you seen a man in a green turban?" and people will *surely* tell us!' Laxman grinned. 'We don't even know his name.'

That afternoon they headed back to the palace road. Then they stood exactly where Nakul had halted the cart and looked around. Across from the palace were three lanes leading off from the main road, and they tried to remember which one the turbaned man had entered. Finally they decided it was the middle one and walked over. It was a quiet lane, with houses on both sides hidden behind high hedges.

'I've heard that all the noblemen live here, around the palace,' Laxman said. 'And the senior ministers and generals too.'

'Well, Green Turban Man was definitely no nobleman. Have you ever seen a nobleman walking instead of riding a chariot?'

'He must work for a nobleman then.'

They strolled along, but the mysterious man in the green turban was nowhere to be found. As Parvati pointed out, if he wore a different turban today, they wouldn't spot him because they never saw his face. The lane now curved to the right and, turning, they saw a man on horseback come out of a large house, leaving the gate open. They peered in and saw a row of rooms around a courtyard, horses tied in a stable and cows chewing cud under a thatched shelter in the corner. It was a busy place, and they watched as many servants scuttled about, carrying jugs and bowls of food from the kitchen as well as baskets and linen from the storeroom.

'Looks like an inn,' said Nakul as they wandered into the courtyard with no one stopping them.

Trying to look casual, they peeked into some of the rooms through small windows, as if they were looking for someone. In the first room, a family was sitting on the floor eating lunch. In the second, a man was asleep on a low bed. The third room was empty, but something made them stop and stare. A pile of discarded clothes lay on the bed, and among them was a familiar green turban!

The three rushed back to the courtyard and looked around. 'We can't spot the man without the turban, Bhaiya!' Parvati said. 'Remember, his face was covered with his turban? All we saw were his eyes.'

'We have to tell Bhikshu Aditya.'

'We don't know where he is—at the vihara or the palace.'

As they stood there, undecided on what to do next, they saw a man walk up to the door of the empty room, use a key to unlock the padlock and then go inside. They got a quick glimpse of a narrow, thin-lipped, moustached face, and the man was wearing quite a lot of jewellery—large silver earrings, a thick bangle and a thin chain around his neck. Today he was not wearing a turban, and his long hair was tied in a knot at the nape of his neck.

Now things were getting even more complicated.

'That must be him! But by the time we get to Bhikshu Aditya, he could go off again!'

'At least we can tell him where the man is staying.'

'Should one of us stay here while the other two go look for Bhikshu Aditya?'

Just then, a boy carrying a thali of food went up to Green Turban Man's door and called out.

The man opened the door and the boy handed the thali to him, collected some money and came away. Then Green Turban Man slammed the door shut.

In a flash Parvati was beside the boy, giving him her most charming smile and asking, 'Please, bhaiya, can you help me? *Please?*'

The boy smiled back. 'If I can.'

'Who is staying in the room to which you delivered the food just now?'

The boy frowned. 'Why do you want to know?'

As Parvati went speechless, for she had no idea what to say next, Nakul quickly stepped in. 'You see, our father has sent us to look for a customer staying in this inn.'

'Customer from where?' The boy smiled again.

'My father is a potter, and a trader from Ujjaini is supposed to be staying here,' Laxman chipped in. 'And we have to take him to the pottery shop. His name is, er . . . Adhiraj!'

'Nah!' The boy shook his head. 'No one from Ujjaini is staying here.' He waved a hand at Green Turban Man's room. 'He is a soldier from Takshashila. Here to meet noblemen in the city and look for work.' Frowning, he added, 'I think his name is Krishanu Singh.'

'Oh!' Laxman tried to look disappointed. 'Then Adhiraj has probably not arrived yet. We'll come again tomorrow.'

Just then, there was a yell from the kitchen and, with another quick smile, the boy hurried away.

The three went back home, loaded some pottery on to the bullock cart and headed to the vihara. They had done enough walking for the day. At the vihara, the guard let them in upon spotting the pottery and, leaving the cart under a tree, they ran to the chaitya, where Aditya was usually found at this time.

The abbot was standing before the altar, and the young monk was with him. Now knowing that he was Prince Mahendra, the children got a bit nervous and hung back until Mahendra spotted them and waved them over with a big smile. 'Ah, my friends!' He turned to Aditya, saying, 'They saved me from a very long and hot walk that morning!'

'We have found the man in the green turban!' Parvati blurted out excitedly.

'Who?' Mahendra looked puzzled.

Aditya, Parvati, Laxman and Nakul first told him the whole story of the mysterious man who had followed the cart, and then the children reported on how they had come across the inn and found the man.

'Following me all the way from Takshashila?' Mahendra looked even more puzzled now. *Why?*

'Do you know anyone named Krishanu Singh?'

Mahendra shook his head.

'We'll find out soon enough!' Aditya announced, striding out of the chaitya and giving orders to a soldier. Soon a chariot rode up to the hall door, and before climbing in, Aditya turned a stern face to Prince Mahendra. 'I am going to report this to His Majesty. Till this mystery is solved, Bhikshu Mahendra, you will NOT step out of the vihara. Am I making myself understood?'

With Mahendra nodding meekly, Laxman said cheekily, 'And we won't give him a ride either!'

'I'll come to your house tomorrow morning, children,' Aditya called as the chariot began to move. 'By then I'll have the whole story. Now, go home!'

The next morning when Aditya came to their door, the three children were waiting impatiently for him, nearly breathless with excitement.

'Did you catch Krishanu Singh?'

'What did he say? Why was he following us?'

'What about the second man?'

'Patience . . . patience . . .' Aditya laughed. He entered the courtyard, and Laxman ran to get him a stool to sit on.

'The soldiers caught him easily. He was asleep in his room and was very surprised at being accused. He is sticking to the story that his name is Krishanu Singh and that he is a soldier from Takshashila who is looking for work in Pataliputra. But he said he was *not* at the vihara that morning, that he has *never* seen Prince Mahendra, that he did *not* follow any bullock cart and that he did *not* meet anyone outside the palace.'

'He did!' Nakul said. 'We all saw him, and Laxman even tried to hear what they were talking about!'

Laxman shrugged. 'I didn't hear much . . . and whatever little I heard made no sense.'

'Still, tell me again.' Aditya leaned forward eagerly. 'Try and remember every word, Laxman. This man is lying and we can all make that out. He is planning something, and we have to keep the prince safe.'

Screwing up his face in concentration, Laxman tried to remember those softly spoken words. 'I think Krishanu was saying that the prince had travelled on a cart with children. Then he asked the other man what he should do next, who said something about reporting to somebody called . . . I think . . . Bhairava.'

Aditya sat up with a frown. 'Bhairava? Are you sure he said Bhairava?'

Laxman nodded. 'That I heard quite clearly. Who is he?'

'There is a retired general in the cavalry called Bhairava Singha. Recently he was sacked by His Majesty because he did not obey orders, and I hear he was very angry.'

'Does he live in the lane where the inn is?'

'I don't know.' Aditya got up. 'We have to meet the *mahamatra* and tell him everything. We'll hire a carriage, let's go!'

'We're coming with you?' Nakul asked, startled.

'Yes! *You* have to tell the mahamatra everything.'

In a flash the children ran inside to tell their parents, while Aditya went out to the main road and hailed a horse-drawn carriage. They all climbed in and went clip-clopping towards the palace. They were so excited they could hardly speak.

'Whom will we meet at the palace, Bhikshu?' Parvati asked.

'Mahamatra Vishnu Sena. He is the minister responsible for guarding the royal family.'

Soon they were at the palace gates and, to the children's amazement, the chariot was allowed in after one look at Aditya. As they rode through the grounds, Laxman, Parvati and Nakul looked around, their eyes dazzled by the beauty of the palace. It had many courtyards, and the ones in front had beautifully painted brick rooms in which the offices were located. Behind another gate were the courtyards where the royal family lived. Everywhere there were gardens, lily ponds and shady trees. The place was bustling with people—men and women hurrying about their work. And there were guards at all the gates and doors.

The mahamatra sat on a thick cushion on the floor, at a low wooden table, reading a pile of reports written on palm leaves. He frowned as he heard Aditya's account and then asked the children a lot of searching questions.

'Ah, of course! I should have guessed Bhairava was behind all this. He is an angry and reckless man, and age has made him stupid. Just because he had served His Majesty's father, King Bindusara, he thought that King Ashoka would never ask him to retire. He never thinks before acting, and I'm sure he has been planning to kidnap the prince. Just the kind of foolish thing he would do!'

With their job done, Aditya and the children now left to relax in a shady veranda on the palace grounds and watch the action. A general in a chariot snapped out orders to a group of soldiers on horseback, and they rode out of the gates with their spears glinting in the sun and their swords swinging at their waists.

By the time the foursome was enjoying bowlfuls of mango juice sent by the mahamatra, the soldiers came back with a man tied to the back of a horse. They looked curiously at Bhairava Singha, a stocky old man with long white hair, a huge moustache and angry eyes that glared at them from under bushy brows. Parvati silently thanked Sakyamuni that the gentle prince Mahendra had not fallen into the hands of this dangerous man.

Later the mahamatra told them that Bhairava's plan had indeed been to kidnap the prince and then get a huge ransom from the king. It was to be his revenge for being sacked from the army. He had decided that Prince Mahendra would be easier to kidnap from the vihara than the well-guarded palace. That morning, Krishanu had been keeping an eye on the vihara to find out if Prince Mahendra had shifted there. But he had been surprised to see the young monk come out on the cart and so he had followed the children to see where the prince was going.

A month later, Laxman, Parvati, Nakul and their families were at the vihara—all in their finest clothes— to watch Prince Mahendra be ordained as a monk. The vihara was decorated with garlands of marigolds for the ceremony and in the chaitya, tall metal lamps were glowing with many flames. The hall was full of guests, all clad in silk, and the women wore so much jewellery that Parvati's eyes were dazzled. His Majesty King Ashoka and all his queens were there and someone pointed out the prince's mother, Queen Mahadevi. At the end of the ceremony, Aditya escorted Queen Mahadevi to the children, and they all bowed low and touched her feet. Putting gold chains around their necks, she thanked them for protecting her son.

Aditya, of course, had the last word as he waved them goodbye at the gate. 'Well, children, it was all very exciting but from tomorrow we go back to studies. Come to the vihara in the afternoon and we will start a new book.'

Parvati made a glum face and everyone laughed.

Historical Note

During the reign of the Mauryan king Ashoka, Buddhism was the main religion of the people, though Ashoka made it clear his subjects were free to follow any religion they wanted. Buddhism attracted the poor because it rejected the caste system, and everyone—from the king to the trader, weaver or potter—was treated as equals. The Brahmins monopolized education and refused to teach girls or the poor, but the Buddhist monks were happy to educate everyone. Even girls were encouraged to learn to read and write, and there are collections of poetry written by Buddhist nuns.

A Lamp for Raavana

Thinking back to that morning, Raghava could never fathom the mystery. On such a quiet, peaceful and ordinary day, what had made his friend Venkata think of a rakshasa king?

It was dawn, and Raghava and Venkata were sitting on the sand, waiting for the fishing boats to return. The sea was calm, with just the regular surge and rise of the grey-green waves tipped with foam splashing over their legs and then sweeping back to the sea again. The sun was barely visible on the horizon, where it was still just a small curve of glowing orange, and the sky was slowly turning a pale grey-blue, the clouds edged with pink.

Then, as the sun rose higher, the boats appeared like moving dots on the horizon and soon they had bobbed up to the shore. The fishermen jumped out and began to haul the boats up the sand, their dark bodies gleaming. These were the fishermen of their village, and the two boys could see their fathers among them.

As the boys started walking towards the sea, Venkata suddenly said, 'You know, if your father had been an actor in a travelling theatre troupe, he would have made a great Raavana.'

A little surprised, Raghava looked closely at his father's broad, sweaty face—with its thick, arched eyebrows over large bloodshot eyes and a moustache curling across his round cheeks—as well as the dark, stocky, muscled body and had to agree. 'He'd be perfect,' he said with a small laugh.

'And he won't even need a false moustache!' Venkata added in a wicked whisper. 'This one is just right.'

'There is the matter of the nine more heads, of course,' Raghava whispered back, and they exchanged a quick grin.

By then they were picking up the baskets of wriggling fish gleaming silver in the sun from the boats and dumping them on the shore.

Seeing them smiling, Raghava's father glared at his son. 'What's so funny?'

'Nothing, Appa.'

Later that morning, as they were working in the vegetable patch behind their home, Raghava told his younger sister, Kanti, what Venkata had said. Kanti, who was busy plucking the dead leaves from the pumpkin vine that had climbed up the roof of their hut, nodded and laughed. 'He is *so* right. To play Raavana, Appa will just have to be himself.' She plucked another yellowed leaf and then added a little grimly, 'He won't need to act much either to be a demon king, will he?'

'No, he won't.'

Raghava and Venkata lived in the land of the Ramayana. Their tiny seaside village was an hour's journey from the temple town of Rameswaram, and across the expanse of the ocean was the island of Lanka, which was once the kingdom of Raavana. It was said in the Ramayana that Lord Rama and his brother Lakshmana had come to Rameswaram while searching for Sita. And that later, they'd built a bridge across the ocean to reach Lanka. Raghava, Venkata and Kanti had visited Rameswaram and wandered around its ancient Ramanatha Swamy Temple, where Lord Rama had worshipped the god Shiva, seeking his blessings before he'd invaded Lanka. Then after his victory, he had come back to perform the funeral rites for Raavana.

Their village depended on Rameswaram, its busy bazaars and its many pilgrims. Every morning, the bullock carts creaked out of their village, laden with baskets of fish and vegetables, sacks of rice and lentils. These were sold in the markets of the pilgrim town, and the carts came back in the evening, carrying cloth and saris, spices and pretty earthen pots.

One autumn evening, a few days before Deepavali, Raghava was lounging near the road when the carts came back. He saw that the first cart had a passenger sitting next to the driver. He was a very old man, wearing a white dhoti with a cotton shawl wrapped about his bare bony body. His long white hair was knotted at the back of his neck and his forehead was streaked with sandalwood paste.

Looks like a priest, Raghava thought, feeling very curious as few people ever visited their village. *Why has he come here? Who is he visiting?*

By the next morning, the news had spread like smoke among the tiny huts along the village's only road. It originated at the temple, where Dhaniamma, the milk-woman, got the details from the village priest, Shankara. Then as she delivered milk from house to house, she passed on the word till everyone knew about the mysterious visitor.

'His name is Harihara, and he is a famous *kathakaar*!'

'He'll be telling the story of the Ramayana at the temple!'

'Shankara says that the landlord Selvam heard him at Kanchipuram and invited him. And did you know

Selvam has promised to pay him TEN gold coins for just three nights of storytelling?'

And finally Dhaniamma came to the headlines. 'Selvam says that this storyteller is very famous. He has sung the Ramayana before our king, His Majesty Raja Raja Chola, at Thanjavur! Impressed, the king gave him a gold bracelet, a bag of coins and a silk shawl!'

To discuss the news, Raghava and Venkata met later in the day under the banyan tree beside the pond.

'Heard about the storyteller?' Raghava asked. 'You know, I saw him when he arrived last evening. He's really old, all stooped and white-haired. Will he be able to sing all night long?'

'Well, if he is such a famous man—a kathakaar to our king and all that—what's he doing in our village?' Venkata wanted to know.

'Selvam is rich—you know that. He can afford to pay ten gold coins for three nights of storytelling. And for a kathakaar that is pretty good money.'

'We have to find a way to go.' Venkata thoughtfully chewed on a blade of grass. 'It starts tonight, doesn't it? Do you think Selvam will invite us?'

'Yes! Everyone is invited.'

Venkata sat up, his eyes wide. *'Really?'*

'And Selvam is feeding everyone *prasadam* too!'

Raghava could barely sit still for the rest of the day. He loved the epic tale of the Ramayana, that amazing saga of Rama, the prince of Ayodhya, who was banished to the forests for fourteen years with his wife, Sita, and brother Lakshmana, because of his evil stepmother Kaikeyi. Then Raavana, the demon king of Lanka, kidnapped Sita, and the two princes went looking for her, having many adventures on the way. Raghava's favourite part of the story was when they met the monkey god, Hanumana, the son of Vayu, or the god of the winds, who flew across the ocean to Lanka in search of Sita.

As Raghava had once said to Venkata, if he had been the son of Vayu, the first place he would have visited would have been Ayodhya, where Rama was born, because he thought Rama was quite wonderful. To him, he was such a heroic figure, a brave warrior, a kind and caring king, and a loving son and brother. For Raghava, Lord Rama was a true hero and his favourite, but Venkata liked Hanumana best—his favourite bit of the story was when Hanumana set fire to Lanka. Of course, both he and Raghava just loved the exciting final battle between Rama and his monkey army and Raavana and his demonic rakshasa forces. They could listen to that story a hundred times and not get bored. And now that a storyteller was going to recite the Ramayana in their village? Raghava, Venkata and Kanti would be there come storm, thunder and lightning or an earthquake—you could be sure of that!

As the sun began to set, the whole village trooped towards the temple. They were all wearing their best clothes, the men in crisp white dhotis and kurtas and the women in their brilliantly coloured saris and with flowers in their hair. As they gathered in the temple courtyard, the air was filled with excited murmurs, with everyone looking around and taking in the scene. They all agreed that Selvam had spared no money for the occasion. Woven mats had been laid on the stone floor and rows of earthen lamps lit in the corners. Incense burned in bowls and flower garlands were wrapped around the pillars. Venkata sniffed happily at the mixed aroma of flowers, incense and burning oil and said it was the smell of festivals.

The storyteller, Harihara, was to sit on a small dais with a tall brass lamp set beside it, and he would play a tambura when he sang.

'He'll only perform for three nights,' Kanti whispered. 'Then he can't recite the whole Ramayana, can he?'

'I don't want to listen to the story of Sita's *swayamvara* again,' Venkata muttered. 'All the kathakaars tell you that one.'

'Well, Deepavali is next week. Do you think we are going to hear the story of the Rama–Raavana battle?' Raghava wondered aloud hopefully.

'Oh, that would be so much more fun!' Kanti nodded happily. 'Raavana roaring and Sita weeping!'

'Kumbhakarna snoring! Hanumana jumping!'

'Rama and Lakshmana covering the sky with their flying arrows!'

Just then, Venkata's uncle, who was sitting in front of them, turned and glared at the children. 'Shut up, you three!' And they stopped their happy Ramayana game.

After they had all eaten the prasadam of delicious sweets and fruits, Selvam got up to welcome the storyteller and, to their joy, he announced that Harihara would tell them the 'Yuddha Kaanda', the story of the great battle! Finally, Harihara stepped up to the dais and bowed low. Today he was wearing a bright-red dhoti, a cream tunic and a tall gold-and-red turban. Raghava looked at the proud figure and thought he appeared very different from the tired old man in the cart. The storyteller sat down and ran his fingers over the strings of the tambura, filling the air with its mellow echoing drone. The three children sat up straight, their eyes wide with anticipation. They were sure this was going to be a great show!

Harihara announced he was going to sing and recite the verses from *Kambar Ramayana*, composed by the great Tamil poet Kamban, and he began his story with Rama, Lakshmana, Sugreeva and Hanumana standing on the seashore in Rameswaram, looking across the waters at Lanka. A bridge had to be built across the ocean, but how would they do it?

Raghava soon realized that Harihara was truly a great kathakaar. Even though he was an old man,

his voice was strong and tuneful when he sang, and the audience swayed with the melody. They listened breathlessly as he described how Raavana went into Ashokavan and threatened Sita, and when he recounted how the helpless Sita began to cry, the women in the audience wept into their saris. When Hanumana set fire to Lanka, there was spontaneous applause, and when the monkeys began to build the bridge, everyone sat up and smiled.

Slowly the earthen lamps guttered and went out, until, finally, the audience was sitting in the dark. Only the tall brass lamp beside Harihara remained lit, the flame standing straight in the still night air. Harihara's face was in light and shadow, his hands making patterns in the air as he wove his magic. His voice had them mesmerized, and it was as if there were an invisible screen behind him on which they could see it all—Rama worshipping Shiva . . . Hanuman flying in with Gandhamadan Hill . . . Sita sitting sadly under a tree . . .

Late into the night, very gradually, Harihara brought the story to a close and said gently, 'This is all for tonight. Tomorrow you will hear the verses on the great battle at Lanka.'

The old man got up a bit stiffly, bowed and stepped off the dais. The audience took a deep breath, as if waking from a trance, and slowly began to head home. Raghava walked back with his head full of music, poetry and dreams.

The next evening, Raghava, Venkata and Kanti were among the earliest to arrive at the temple and got seats in the front. Soon the battle was in full swing, and Harihara's voice was high with excitement as he described the sounds of war—the twang of Rama's great bow and the whoosh of the shower of arrows that streaked across the sky; the clash of swords, maces and battleaxes; the cries of pain; and the shouts of triumph.

By the end of the night, Kumbhakarna and Indrajit were dead, and Raavana himself was coming to the battlefield to fight. Then, raising his voice, Harihara began to describe the magnificent king of the rakshasas.

'There he came, the great Raavana, flying in on his Pushpaka rath—and it was an awesome sight! He was a great scholar and a devotee of Shiva, who composed Sanskrit *shloka*s and knew the Vedas. But today he was a king and a warrior, wearing red clothes, golden armour and a tall crown. His twenty arms held many kinds of weapons and his ten heads made a fearful sight, the faces full of rage, the eyes red and rolling...'

That's when, out of the blue, Raghava remembered that joke Venkata had made about his appa. The way Harihara was describing Raavana, it was as if he were describing his father on those nights when he came home late, swaying and shouting, drunk on rice liquor. His appa was no longer human when he was drunk—he became a demon. On some nights, Raghava, Kanti and their amma went and hid in the fields to avoid him because when he drank, everything made him angry. He was always sorry the next day and it did not happen very often, but Raghava was truly afraid of his father's rages on those dark, terrible nights.

With a quick shake of his head, Raghava pushed away those images and tried to listen to the storyteller again. As Raavana came roaring on to the battlefield, the great contest between Rama and Raavana began, and soon he had forgotten about his appa.

The following afternoon, Raghava went looking for Harihara and found the old man sitting on the beach under the shade of a palm tree, chewing paan and staring out to sea. No one was around, and it was very quiet except for the rhythmic crash of the waves and the rustling of the palm fronds.

Raghava bent his head in a namaskar and said, 'Sir, you are a great storyteller!'

The old man looked up and smiled. 'You were sitting in the front last night. You liked the story of the battle, hmm?'

'Oh yes!'

The lined, old eyes were gentle. 'What's your name?'

'Raghava.'

'Ah! You are named after Lord Rama! He is also called Raghava, because he belonged to the clan of the Raghus. Did you know that?'

Raghava nodded and then, trying to sound casual, said, 'Sir, you called Raavana a great scholar, but how can that be? He was a rakshasa . . . and demons are evil, aren't they?'

Harihara turned to look at the boy as if his question had surprised him. 'Raavana's father was the sage Vishrava, so he was a Brahmin. He studied with his father, became very learned and knew all the sacred books.'

'But wasn't he the king of the rakshasas?'

'His mother, Kaikasi, was from the rakshasa tribe.' The old man gave a slight smile. 'You know, rakshasas were human, like us. They were just not from the same clan as Rama and Lakshmana. They probably looked different, had dark skin and curly hair—but they didn't really have fangs, green skin or long nails.'

'Of course they did!' Raghava protested.

Harihara shook his head. 'In the story they are the enemy, so to make them seem even more terrible, the storytellers made them ugly too. If you go to Lanka, you will find people just like us living there. Also, don't forget, there were many good rakshasas too.'

'Who? Surpanakha?' Raghava asked a little sarcastically.

Harihara laughed. 'Well, no . . . though you should feel a little sorry for her. She did lose her nose, poor woman! Let's see . . . there was Raavana's queen Mandodari, who was very beautiful and also a wise and good person. Then don't forget Vibhishana—as Raavana's brother, he should have had fangs too, but he didn't. The storytellers only made him good-looking because he was on Rama's side!'

Raghava nodded thoughtfully. 'I do, sort of like Kumbhakarna...'

'You know Kumbhakarna did not approve of what Raavana was doing, don't you? He told his brother to send Sita back, but Raavana wouldn't listen to him.'

They sat in companionable silence for some time and then Raghava asked, 'What about Raavana's ten heads?'

'That again is a poet's imagery to show how intelligent and talented he was. Raavana was not just a scholar but also a warrior, and he was a powerful king and Lanka was a prosperous kingdom. It is said he could recite all the Vedas from memory and was a good poet, who composed shlokas in praise of Shiva. I know of one called the "Shiva Tandava Stotra".'

'And ... if you have ten heads, I suppose you *do* need twenty arms.'

Harihara laughed. 'Very true—to hold all those weapons!'

'But, sir, if he was so intelligent, why did he kidnap Sita?' Raghava turned a puzzled face towards Harihara. 'That was not what a great man would do.'

'Once you grow up and read the Ramayana, you'll realize that no one is perfect. They all have good qualities and bad ones, strengths and weaknesses. They all make mistakes. That is why it is such a great epic.'

'Bad qualities? *Even Rama?* You must be joking!' Raghava protested hotly. 'He fought a demon king with just a small army, *and* he won. Lord Rama was so brave!'

'Yes, he is Purushottama, the perfect being, but even he made mistakes. Think about it.'

Raghava, who knew the Ramayana well, thought for a moment and then said reluctantly, 'Well . . . he shouldn't have killed Vali the way he did, hiding and attacking him from the back. That was not fair.'

'And neither was the killing of Indrajit. He was at his prayers and did not have his weapons with him.'

Raghava nodded as he absently drew a complicated pattern in the sand. 'So even Raavana is not all bad. Is that what you are saying?'

'Well, he was more bad than good. His greatest weakness was his pride and arrogance. He thought that he could do anything, even if it was wrong, and that he would get away with it. For all his learning, he was selfish, cruel and greedy.'

'And he thought he could defeat Rama! That was even more stupid!'

'Like many rich and powerful men, he thought he was invincible, but then just one arrow from Rama's bow killed him and there he lay, in the dust . . .'

The two of them sat looking out to sea in a friendly silence. Raghava suddenly thought of the day the week before, when his appa had gone to Rameswaram and made good money from selling the fish. He had come back with a bundle of new clothes for Kanti, Raghava and their amma. He had also got packets of spices, a box of sweets, a new brass water pot, a doll for Kanti and a tin sword for Raghava. Their amma had laughed and protested that he had spent all his money on the Deepavali gifts but not brought anything for himself, and he'd just sat there, grinning happily, as Raghava and Kanti had danced around him.

'So,' Raghava said thoughtfully, 'no one's perfect.'

The old man looked sharply at the solemn young face beside him and agreed gently, 'No one's perfect. We can only try to be good.'

Then Raghava remembered what his amma had said to his appa: 'It would be the best gift for your family if you stopped drinking.'

'You turn into a demon . . .' Kanti had said softly.

'We get so scared, Appa,' Raghava had added.

Raghava had been amazed to see his father suddenly look ashamed. 'I promise I'll stop drinking . . . I know I have hurt you all.'

So, as the old man said, maybe his appa would now try to be good. Raghava could at least hope.

A few days later, it was Deepavali. As the sun set, Kanti and Raghava lit lamps and placed them around their hut. The rows of tiny earthen lamps were like golden garlands of light that turned their simple home into a glowing palace.

Then Raghava took one large lamp, filled it with oil and dipped a cotton wick in it. He took the lamp and placed it on the threshold of their home and, lighting it, said softly to himself, 'Raavana, this one's for you.'

Historical Note

Rameswaram in Tamil Nadu is the place where Lord Rama, helped by Hanumana and his monkey army, built the bridge to Raavana's kingdom of Lanka. It is home to the famous Ramanatha Swamy Temple, which stands at the site where Rama performed the funeral rites of Raavana after the battle. Pilgrims have been going to this sacred place for centuries and keep the memories of the Ramayana alive.

DHANI

His day began and ended at the river. At dawn, as the sky lightened in the east and the birds flew over his head, welcoming the new day, he would walk down the steps of the ghat to the water. Then, as he stood reciting the 'Gayatri Mantra', the river would be all around him, the water rising to his waist in a cool, living presence.

In the evening, he went back home across the darkening waters just as the lamps were lit in the temples by the ghats and the sound of the temple bells came echoing towards his boat.

The river was always with him.

Pandit Kalpeshwar Tripathi could not imagine life without the presence of River Ganga. In Kashi, they'd say that the city was the kingdom of Lord Shiva, but for him it was the flowing waters of the Ganga that spelled home. When he sat and watched her waters flow over the steps of the ghat like a liquid benediction, he knew that he was in a sacred space.

That morning, as always, Kalpeshwar was on his way from Kedar Ghat, where he lived, to Assi Ghat, where he taught in a pathshala attached to the Sankat Mochan Temple. Recently, many new pathshalas had been opened in Kashi under the patronage of Maharaja Prasenajit, the king of Kashi and Kosala. However, Kalpeshwar's school was an old one and he had been teaching there for nearly thirty years. What he liked most about it was that a patch of the river was visible from the doorway of his classroom.

And on this river, he was now sitting at one end of the boat that was being rowed by his regular boatman, Dhani. He would be waiting for the teacher in the evening to bring him back home. Kalpeshwar, careful of his purity as a Brahmin, made sure that he sat far away from the defiling shadow of the low-caste Dhani, but that did not stop them from chatting.

Dhani liked to talk and the pandit liked to answer his questions. He found talking to the boy to be oddly peaceful.

'How old are you, Dhani?' he asked

'I don't really know, Panditji.' The boy shrugged, his dark, muscled shoulders straining at the oars. 'Amma only remembers that it was during the rains, and that it was the year the river covered all the steps of Dasaswamedha Ghat.'

The old pandit laughed and then studied the dusky, sharp-featured face before him. 'I think you are fifteen or sixteen. I remember your father telling me he'd had a son. He always gave me all the family news.'

'Maybe.' The boy shrugged indifferently again. 'Does it really matter? I am a boatman today, and I'll be rowing till the day I die.' He gave a quick sigh. 'Just like my father and his father before him.'

'How is your father?'

'He can walk now but I don't think he'll be able to row a boat any time soon.'

Some months ago, Dhani's father had slipped on the steps of a ghat and hurt his head, so now young Dhani was the only breadwinner of the family. Soon after the accident, one morning, Dhani had offered Kalpeshwar some money for a puja for his father. The pandit had refused to take it and had instead given the boy a silver coin, saying, 'Use this for his medicines.'

'What about the puja?' Dhani had asked.

'Pujas can wait. The gods don't need to be bribed with pujas. If they truly want the best for us, their devotees, they will listen to our prayers.'

Dhani had given him a startled glance. 'But at the temple, all the priests ask for money.'

'I'm not a priest, I'm a teacher,' Kalpeshwar had replied.

The boy had flashed him a doubtful look. 'The priest says only he can talk to the gods. When you pray, do the gods listen to you too?'

Kalpeshwar had stared across the river and then said gently, 'I think we should not depend too much on the gods. The medicines from the vaid are much more dependable...'

Dhani had smiled and given a quick nod of his curly head. 'Amma wanted the puja. I didn't.'

As the boat now moved across the wide expanse of the Ganga towards Assi, which was the last of the eighty-odd ghats of Kashi, they sat in easy silence. Then, as he often did, Kalpeshwar began to sing, softly chanting one of his favourite shlokas to Shiva—the 'Mahamrityunjaya Mantra'.

Om trayambakam yaja mahe,
Sugandham pushti vardhanam...

As he was reciting the Sanskrit mantra, Kalpeshwar realized there was a soft echo that followed his voice.

Urva rukmiva bandhanan
Mrityor mokshay...

He looked in surprise at Dhani and realized that the boy was reciting with him, and so they sang together till the end. He was so delighted to find the boy singing with him that Kalpeshwar forgot to protest about an outcaste boatman singing in Sanskrit. Any other Brahmin would have been furious at Dhani's audacity.

Kalpeshwar asked, 'How did you learn the shloka?'

'From you, Panditji. You sing every morning in my boat.'

'You learnt just by listening to me?'

Dhani shrugged. 'I remember things . . .'

'Things?'

Dhani stopped rowing, letting the boat drift as he tried to explain. 'I don't know . . . I just don't forget anything I've heard a few times. I know many of the songs that you sing.' And to Kalpeshwar's astonishment, Dhani then sang snatches of the many mantras that he'd sing in the boat on his way to his school.

'How do you remember them? Do you write them down and then memorize them?'

Dhani shook his head. 'I can't write too well, so I just listen.' Then he stared at Kalpeshwar, his eyes wide and watchful, and asked nervously, 'Do you think you could teach me to read and write, Panditji?'

Pandit Kalpeshwar Tripathi looked at the pleading young face before him and could not say, 'I only teach high-caste boys, and you are a boatman's son. I cannot teach you because if I do, my community of Brahmins will banish me from the pathshala.' Instead, he just said gently, 'I'll think about it, Dhani.'

'It'll be easy to teach me, Panditji!' A smile curved Dhani's lips. 'You just have to tell me once and I'll remember.' His eyes deepened with a touch of sadness. 'There is a new pathshala near my house and I went there, but the pandit said I'm not of a high caste and so I can't study there. He said that if I went and sat in his classroom, then the other boys won't sit with me.' With a quick cheeky grin, he added, 'But you could teach me in the boat!'

Kalpeshwar laughed. 'Yes, I could do that.'

By then they were at Assi Ghat, and as Dhani held the boat steady, the old pandit carefully stepped on to the slippery mud bank. He brought out a few copper *daam* coins and dropped them from a height into Dhani's outstretched hand, careful that he did not touch him.

A week later, one morning Kalpeshwar was sitting before his class of a dozen Brahmin boys who were being taught the scriptures so that they could become priests. The row of boys had shaven heads with pigtails and wore white dhotis and prominently displayed loops of sacred thread across their chests. They sat bent over their palm-leaf pages, reading aloud, swaying and memorizing.

I try so hard to make them understand the shlokas, appreciate the beauty of the words, but all they want to do is memorize so that they can spout them before a yagna fire. All this effort is only to make a living, he thought sadly.

He turned to look out of the door and catch a glimpse of the Ganga and remembered his conversations with Dhani. The boy had wanted to know the meaning of the mantras that he had picked up, and as Kalpeshwar had explained the significance of the 'Mahamrityunjaya Mantra', he had listened carefully and then given a happy sigh, saying softly, 'It's so beautiful, Panditji! This is real poetry.'

Dhani's mind was filled with questions. He wanted to know where the Ganga started and where it ended. He listened with wide-eyed concentration as Kalpeshwar described the Himalayas and the sea at Ganga Sagar, at the end of the river's journey. He was curious about everything: Why did mangoes grow only in summer and not winter, when onions grew all year round? Had Kalpeshwar seen Pataliputra, where King Bimbisara ruled? Was the sun made of fire?

At times, the old teacher would have to shake his head and confess that he did not have the answer. Dhani knew many of the answers lay in books and that was why he wanted to read—if only Kalpeshwar would teach him. Somehow, to his logical young mind, it made no sense that a mantra could be defiled if he sang it. He was a human being too, wasn't he?

When he sings the mantras with me, with such love and joy, Kalpeshwar brooded, *the mantras sound like music and poetry. They are not defiled by his young, loving voice. It is so much better than this obedient, mechanical repetition that I am hearing now.*

Then a thought struck him: *What am I first? A Brahmin priest or a teacher?* And Kalpeshwar did not have an answer.

That night Kalpeshwar Tripathi could not sleep as Dhani's pleading young face kept floating before his eyes. He got up and left the house, walking through the narrow lanes to Kedar Ghat. He sat down on a step before the Kedareshwar Temple. It was still dark, and the ghat, quiet and empty. The early-morning bathers would start arriving closer to dawn. It was so silent that he could hear the soft splashing of the river hitting the steps of the ghat. The Ganga was a dark, glistening expanse before him, catching patches of the fading moonlight. The still air carried a faint aroma of flowers and incense and the slightly dank smell of the river.

The old pandit had come to his river goddess, seeking an answer. The Ganga had to tell him what he was first—a priest or a teacher.

That morning Dhani had asked him a question that haunted him still. 'Panditji, who created the rule that says that you are a Brahmin because you're a teacher and I am an outcaste because I row a boat? Which god said that?'

'No god said it. It is the Brahmins who made the rules.'

'But they are human beings like me.'

'Yes, they are.'

'Then why can't they change the rules?'

'Why should they? The varna system makes them powerful and rich. They say the gods told them about varna and jati, and that they obey the gods.'

'You are a Brahmin. Did the gods tell you that?' Dhani had asked.

Kalpeshwar had laughed. 'No, they did not. I did not hear anything from the gods and I'm quite sure the others did not either.' He could not tell a lie to the dark pain in those young eyes. 'These are all just stories we make up to make money.'

Now Kalpeshwar thought back to the years of teaching and realized that what he remembered the most were the good students and the joy of teaching them. There was the boy who was a brilliant mathematician and now worked in the royal treasury. Another who composed poetry and had become a famous singer. The boy who'd studied Ayurveda and now practised as a vaid. With Dhani, he felt the same happiness that he had felt while teaching them.

In all the years, though, he had never found a mind like Dhani's. There was the quick understanding, the crystal clear logical reasoning and that extraordinary memory. But most of all, there was that hunger to learn and the passion to discover. Where did he learn to ask those questions?

He knew that Dhani had been seeking teachers all his life. He had once persuaded a grocer to teach him numbers, and now he could calculate quickly in his head. A trader who lived in his lane had taught him the Devanagari alphabet, and so he could recite the letters and even scribble them on the ground with a stick—but it went no further because he had no books to help him read.

Kalpeshwar knew he would have to find a way to teach Dhani, and not on the boat, as the boy had optimistically suggested. *I can hire him as a servant,* he plotted, *to help me with the chores around the house, and I'll teach him when no one is around. My wife is dead, and I am growing old. I live alone and need help.* Then he thought firmly, *Who will know what I do at home?*

As the sun rose, touching the ripples of water with gold, the river gave her answer. The Ganga did not know of the divisions that humans made within themselves. Her waters, fish and clay were for everyone. The water and clay could be used by a Brahmin for his rituals as well as by a potter to mould an *arati* lamp. A weaver dipped his skeins of cotton in her water to dye them in the colours of the rainbow, a farmer irrigated his fields with her supply and fishermen threw their nets across her waters for their daily catch.

Potters, weavers, farmers, fishermen, boatmen . . . these people are the anchors of our lives, and we treat them with such terrible contempt, thought Kalpeshwar. *The river goddess cares for them all with generosity and equality because she is* jeevan-dayini *Ganga. She just knows how to give life.*

'I am a teacher,' Kalpeshwar Tripathi said firmly to himself, 'and I give knowledge. That is my only identity.'

Then walking peacefully back home after his morning bath, he thought with amusement, *I am no longer his panditji. Dhani will now have to call me Guruji. And we just have to find a way to fool the world and its absurd, inhuman, cruel rules.*

Then Kalpeshwar Tripathi threw back his head and laughed. 'I think we'll enjoy the journey.'

Historical Note

You may wonder what children learnt in the pathshalas. Education was limited to the Brahmins and the rich, and it was only for boys. They were taught reading, writing, some Sanskrit, history, logic and theology. No science and, surprisingly, no geography were in the curriculum. Our caste system kept children of the poor, like weavers, potters and carvers, away from education and discouraged enterprise, and it was one of the causes of our backwardness in science and technology.

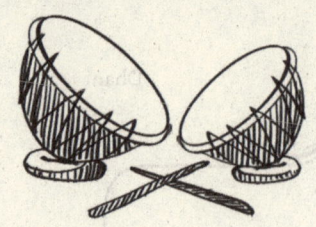

THE CALL OF THUNDER

In the village of Dirmaur they had a saying, 'When the peacocks stop dancing, the rain clouds stay away.'

For two long years Dhaani and his friend Sarju had not seen a peacock dance. Not one. And the rain clouds had stayed away.

Their village was at the edge of the Thar Desert in Rajasthan, but the people had worked hard to keep it green. They had planted trees everywhere, and soon there was a small forest where herds of deer lived. They had dug wells and ponds to catch every drop of rainwater. They had done all they could to keep the desert sands away, but what could they do if the rains did not come?

Dhaani and Sarju were sitting by their pond.

'The water is down to half,' Sarju said gloomily. 'If it doesn't rain soon, the cows will start to die.'

'The crop of jowar in our fields is beginning to droop and turn brown. Soon it will die too.' Dhaani sighed sadly.

'I wish there was some kind of magic that could bring rain,' Sarju said moodily.

'Magic?'

'You know, a magic spell or something. You recite the spell and boom! The clouds come rushing here and it starts to rain.'

'Imagine a magic spell,' Dhaani dreamt as he watched an eagle soar across the sky, 'to make you fly, or one to find hidden treasures!'

'A mantra to find out what Panditji plans to ask us in the maths test . . .' added Sarju.

'To get marbles and kites . . .' And they dreamt on.

Suddenly Dhaani sat up. 'Maybe Ranno Dadi will know about magic spells. Want to go and ask her?'

'No harm in asking but, I'm warning you, if she tries to make me take that horrible brown powder again, I'll leave!'

Everyone in the village knew Ranno Dadi. She lived in a small hut near the Shiva temple and spent her days sitting by the temple door, where people came to meet her. She made powders and syrups for coughs and fevers, stomach aches and painful knees, and she also knew about babies and could read palms.

She was really, really old, and once Dhaani had tried to count the number of wrinkles on her face until she'd finally hit him with her walking stick. Sarju often wondered how she ate because she only had five teeth. Though Ranno Dadi was old, she was no fool. Her small, beady eyes were sharp, and she heard everything and forgot nothing. She was the wise woman of Dirmaur after all.

The boys found Ranno Dadi sitting on her *charpai* with a pile of leaves, berries and tree bark that she was plucking and breaking. She'd picked them from the forest to make her herbal medicines. She looked up with a frown as the boys clambered up to sit beside her.

'Now what do you two monkeys want?' she asked suspiciously and then peered at Sarju. 'How's the cold? Want some more powder?'

'No, thank you, Dadi. My cold is fine!' Sarju said hurriedly. 'Actually, Dadi . . . umm . . . we came to ask you something . . .'

'Don't mumble, Sarju!' Dadi glared at him. 'What is it?'

'Do you know any magic spells?' Dhaani asked quickly.

Dadi sat up. 'Magic spells? Of course not! What do you think I am? A witch?'

'No . . . no . . .' Sarju backtracked. 'But you are *sooo* wise, no? You cured my cough *and* read my palms *and*—'

'Don't you know any magic spells or mantras to bring rain?' Dhaani came straight to the point.

'Rain? Hah! Why should the rain gods listen to me?'

'Who are these rain gods?'

'There are two of 'em—that Indra and Varuna, and they listen to no one. They just go and rain anywhere they like.'

'Stupid, are they?'

'Very! They have no sense at all! Here we are, with no rain for two years, and they are off starting floods somewhere and washing away villages. So praying to them is a waste of time. What we have to do is talk directly to the rain clouds.'

'We can *talk* to clouds?' The boys leaned forward eagerly. *'How?'*

'With thunder, of course!' She glared at them. 'Don't you know anything? You make the thunder and it calls the rain clouds.'

'Make thunder?' Dhaani's eyebrows were rising higher and higher. 'How can you do that?'

Dadi sat back with a small smile curving her lips. 'You see, the rain clouds are in love with thunder, and they will follow the thunder wherever it goes! Haven't you noticed? First there is the sound of thunder and then the rain.' The boys nodded. 'So we have to make thunder above our village, and the monsoon clouds, filled with water, will come floating across the sky because *they are in love!* And then it will rain.'

Dhaani thought that this was the most fantastic fairy tale he had ever heard, but before he could say so, Sarju was asking eagerly, 'Oh, Dadi, then let's make thunder! How do we do that?'

'How should I know?' Dadi shrugged. 'I'm the medicine woman, not a rain man.' Then, looking at their disappointed faces, she said, 'Go and ask Shankar Singh Solanki. He knows how to make thunder.'

'Who?' The boys had never heard of a Shankar Singh Solanki before.

'He lives in the next village—the one with a hill and that old fort in which that mad zamindar lives. And oh! Shankar Singh has a moustache.'

'Every man in Rajasthan has a moustache.' Sarju shrugged.

'Ah!' Ranno Dadi laughed. 'His is special!'

So early next morning, Dhaani and Sarju went looking for a man named Shankar Singh Solanki, who had a special moustache and lived in the village with the old fort and could make thunder. They walked through the forest, where the deer peered at them from behind the trees with their large dark eyes, squirrels ran up and down the tree trunks and sparrows hopped about among the leaves.

'No dancing peacocks,' said Dhaani sadly.

'And if it doesn't rain, this forest will die too,' added Sarju.

'And the desert will take over our village.'

It was nearly noon, the hot sun glaring down on them from a cloudless sky, when they reached the village of Batheri and asked for Shankar Singh Solanki.

'That house by the *keekar* tree.' The shepherd herding a bunch of goats pointed ahead. 'You can't miss it.'

'We can't?'

'You'll hear him.' The shepherd grinned under his huge white turban. 'Shankar Singh is very noisy.'

As they got closer to the small whitewashed house, they understood. They could hear the drumming echoing across the lane.

Dhoooom . . . tat-tat . . . DHOOM!

The boys exchanged a smile—it did sound like thunder.

They peeped through the door into a courtyard, where a man sat on a wooden bed with two drums before him. Shankar Singh was an old man, with his long white hair tied in a knot and such big white moustaches that they curled right across his plump cheeks. He was playing with his eyes closed and only his hands were moving.

Dhoooom! Tat-tat-tat . . . dhoooom!

The boys must have made a noise because he stopped, opened his eyes and asked in a voice as deep as his drums, 'And who are you?'

'I'm Dhaani. This is Sarju, and we have come from Dirmaur to meet you, sir.'

'You have?' Shankar put down his sticks. 'Why?'

'Ranno Dadi sent us. She said the only person in Rajasthan who can make thunder is Shankar Singh Solanki.'

Shankar looked pleased, a smile peeking through his moustache. 'Ranno Bua said that?'

'Bua? She is your *aunt*?' asked Sarju, very surprised.

And Dhaani swallowed a laugh. *Imagine! This old man has an aunt?*

'Yes. And she is the only one who knows about the magic of making thunder. It's a family secret, you see. Now, why do you want me to do that?'

'We need rain.'

'True, so we do. But, boys, I must warn you, it is very, *very* difficult to make thunder. It has to sound like real thunder, or the clouds won't follow. I don't always succeed. Many times the thunder does not work and the rain clouds stay away, and then people get angry with me. So I don't do it any more.'

'It's difficult, is it? Making thunder?' Sarju asked sympathetically.

'Very! It has to sound like the rumble of real thunder, and it has to be so loud that it echoes across the sky and the clouds can hear it even if they are hundreds of miles away. So I can't do it alone—I'll need two more nagara players.'

'Nagara?' Sarju frowned.

'These drums, you fool!' Shankar's moustaches quivered angrily. 'Don't you know anything? Only nagara drums can make thunder, and it can only work when the drummers know how to play really well.'

The boys studied the drums as Shankar told them how in ancient times when kings went to war, the army marched to the beat of the nagaras. And in the palaces of the great Rajput kings, they played the nagaras in the gateway to announce the time. Royal processions were always led by the nagara players.

Nagaras came in pairs. There was a large triangular wooden drum wrapped in a criss-cross of strings and a smaller one made of shiny metal. The smaller one, said Shankar, was a 'lady drum' and made the sharp *tap-tap-tat-tat* noise. The bigger one was a 'man drum' and followed with the loud *booom-dhooom!*

'The smaller one dances.' Dhaani tapped it softly with the drumsticks. *Tip ... tap ... tat ...*

'The big one marches!' And Sarju hit it hard, making it echo across the courtyard. *Dhoooommm!*

'Want to learn?' Shankar asked, and the boys nodded eagerly. 'Get the drums from the room there.'

They ran inside the hut and got another set of drums. Then they learnt the beat of the nagara—*dhoom...tat...tat...dhoooom...tat-tat-tat...booom!*

'You're not bad,' Shankar commented.

'We play the dholak at home.' Dhaani grinned. 'But these nagaras . . . Oof, Chacha! They are magical drums.'

By then it was lunchtime, and Shankar's wife came out with shiny brass thalis laden with thick bajra rotis dripping with fragrant ghee, bowls of dal, a sabji of spinach and potatoes, and crisp onion pakoras. The boys had walked all morning and were very hungry, and they ate and ate . . .

Dhaani gave a happy burp and asked, 'Chacha, where can we find two good nagara players?'

'You'll have to wait. My two sons have gone to play at the Pushkar Mela. They'll be back next week.'

'Then you'll come to our village?'

'I will.'

'You promise?'

'I have to, or Ranno Bua will kill me!'

It was the longest and most anxious week of their life. And the other boys in the village kept teasing them, and that made it even harder.

'A drummer bringing rain? Who's ever heard of that?'

'Clouds falling in love! What is this, nautanki?'

'And what about lightning? How will he make that? With oil lamps?'

And, ho-ho . . . ha-ha, they all laughed.

'Very funny!' Dhaani glared at them. 'And when it rains, I'll drown the lot of you in the pond!'

Oddly enough, the older people took them seriously. Mangey Lal, the sarpanch, decided to have a havan and puja, and Girdhari, the temple priest, pulled out some special mantras to Indra and Varuna. The women cleaned out the temple courtyard, added a new layer of cow dung mixed with earth and decorated it with rangoli patterns in white.

They were ready to try anything for rain.

Exactly a week later, an old bullock cart came creaking down the road, and there was Shankar, sitting in the back and waving at them.

'Who does he think he is?' someone asked. 'Waving like a local maharaja!'

'He can bring rain,' Ranno Dadi said tartly. 'Can your maharaja do that?'

'Hah! Some hope!' said Mangey Lal. 'They can't even build a road!'

Meanwhile, Shankar Singh Solanki and his sons stood before them looking magnificent. They all wore snow-white dhoti–kurtas, and their brightly coloured turbans flared high over their heads. When they spotted Ranno Bua, they rushed to touch her feet.

Soon the nagara players sat cross-legged in a row, with their nagara drums before them. Their many-hued *bandhani* turbans—orange and green, purple and red—were glowing in the afternoon sun. All three had moustaches, but Shankar Singh's was the finest, curving and pointed like the pride of a true Rajput.

Girdhari did his havan and puja—the fragrance of incense perfumed the air and the smoke from the havan fire rose to the sky, carrying their prayers to Indra and Varuna. Then, as the sun began to dip to the west, the nagara players raised their sticks to their forehead, whispered a prayer and began to play.

Dhooooooom!

In the beginning, it was a soft and slow beat, a *tat-tat-taaaat-dhoom!* Then it got faster and faster, and their sticks were flying across the drums, and it got louder and louder and Sarju thought, *It really does sound like thunder . . . I can feel it go BOOM-BOOM in my chest!*

Are they loud enough? Dhaani wondered. *Can the rain clouds hear them?*

Swaying to the beat, Sarju turned and saw something that made him sit up. Right at the edge of the forest a herd of deer stood still, as if they were also listening to the nagaras. And what was *that*? He poked Dhaani and pointed. Wasn't that a peacock strutting up to sit on the temple wall?

DHOOOOM…booom…tat-tat-tat…DHOOOOM! went the nagara drums.

Sarju screwed up his eyes—was he imagining it or was that a patch of grey in the western sky?

Suddenly the sun vanished and a cool breeze began to blow, bending the branches of the keekar trees. The patch of grey began to get bigger and bigger and came rushing towards them, as if the clouds were now so in love that they wanted to be near the thunder of the nagaras.

Ranno Dadi was pointing and laughing. 'See? See?'

Smiles split the faces of the nagara players, and now their hands were moving so fast you only saw a blur and the sound was getting louder and louder…

DHOOOOM!…Tat-tat-tat…DHOOOOMMMM! The clouds had covered the sky, and the first raindrops came splashing down over a row of happy, laughing faces. The rain fell on the trees, turning their dusty leaves all shiny and green again. The stony courtyard was now beautifully muddy as puddles of water began to collect all around. And on the wall, the peacock opened its shiny blue-gold-purple tail and began to dance! And the children began to dance too.

First there was a flash of silver lightning that went zigzagging across the sky, and then there was the roll of real thunder that seemed to move to the beat of the nagara drums. Finally, the skies opened up and the rain came pouring down.

Dhooooom! CRACK! CRACK! RUMMMBLE . . . DHOOOOOM!

Everyone was now laughing, singing and dancing and getting soaking wet, and the three great thunder-makers, the magical nagara players—their turbans drenched, faces streaming with rain—played on and on . . .

Historical Note

Rajasthan has the Thar Desert and gets very little rain, and so the people dance, sing and play on their drums to pray for rain. Over the centuries, they have developed many ingenious ways to store water, like check dams and ponds called *talav*s that are being revived today. Some of the old fortresses, like Mehrangarh in Jodhpur, have many clever ways of saving every drop of rainwater.

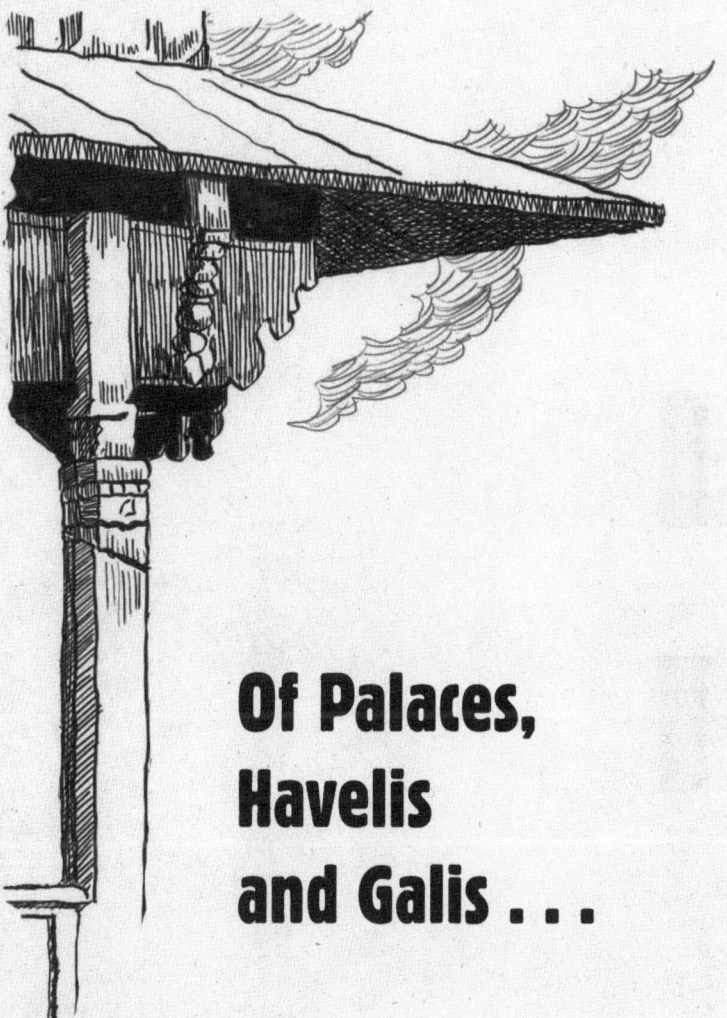

Of Palaces,
Havelis
and Galis . . .

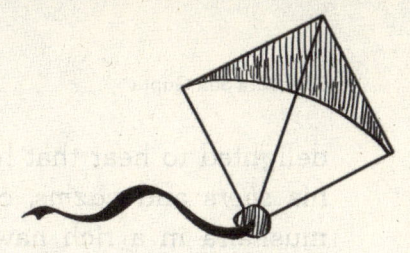

A Sherwani for Abbu

'You'll need a new sherwani,' Mushir's ammi said to his abbu.

'And what about a pair of *jootis*?' asked his elder sister, Raunaq. 'You know those shoes with gold zari embroidery on top?'

'And a silk cap,' Mushir added a final touch to his father's wardrobe.

Ahmed Hasan 'Dehlvi' smiled gently at his family and shook his head. 'My old sherwani will have to do.' For him, new clothes were an impossible dream. For what he earned teaching at the local madrasa barely paid the bills and often by the end of the month, he would have to borrow money from friends.

But Mushir's father, Ahmed Hasan, was not just a teacher of Urdu, he was also a poet—a well-known *shair* of Delhi. That morning, his family had been delighted to hear that he had been invited to recite his *sher*s and *nazm*s, couplets and songs, at a big mushaira in a rich nawab's house. Everyone knew that this nawab only invited the best poets of the city to his cultural gatherings. Mushir and Raunaq had danced in delight at hearing the news! Finally, their abbu was going to get the respect that he deserved. Also, at these mushairas, the poets were paid well, and if their abbu could recite something that pleased the audience then there would be more awards.

Just then, Mushir's and Raunaq's eyes fell on their abbu's old sherwani hanging from a nail on the wall. The sleeves of the long coat were frayed, there was a patch at one elbow and the cloth had become shiny from many washings. He couldn't possible stand on stage before hundreds of people to recite his poetry wearing that!

That afternoon, after lessons at the madrasa, Mushir and his best friend, Abbas, were busy playing with marbles in their lane, but Mushir was still thinking about the problem of the sherwani.

Taking careful aim at a blue marble, he said thoughtfully, 'It's funny, really . . . Our *badshah* is a shair himself. He writes poetry as Bahadur Shah 'Zafar' and in his kingdom, a good poet like Abbu can't afford a new sherwani.'

'You have to be Mirza Ghalib to be able to afford new clothes.' Abbas shrugged. 'And what can the old badshah do? His kingdom is just this city of Delhi, and even that is really ruled by the gora English army. He's a poor old man and lives on a pension given by the goras!' With a flick of his wrist, Abbas aimed at a milky-green marble and missed.

Mushir, now distracted from the game, tried to imagine the mushaira: It would be a glittering occasion in the nawab's courtyard, under a brightly coloured tent. There would be tall lamps glowing in the corners, rich silk carpets on the floor with velvet bolsters to lean on. The entrance would be decorated with rose, jasmine and marigold garlands, and the air would be fragrant with the smoke of incense. The gathering would be of the powerful nobles of the city, all clad in silks and jewels, and the exquisitely dressed women would be sitting behind chick curtains. Mushir remembered his abbu telling them that great poets like Ghalib and Zauq sahib had been invited as well. So now he imagined his abbu, sitting quietly in a corner, trying to hide the frayed sleeves of his sherwani, wearing old shoes and a cloth cap. Mushir couldn't bear the picture.

'Look!' Abbas was staring up at the sky. 'The mad old nawab is flying his gold-tailed kite again.'

Everyone knew about Nawab Bakhtiar Khan, an eccentric old nawab who lived in their lane in Ballimaran, and his famous kite battles with his enemy Bulle Khan. All the nawab ever wanted to do was fly kites, and he spent a lot of money on them. His kites always had a tail made of real gold zari! All the boys in the mohalla kept an eye out for the nawab's kite, because if it was cut, whoever caught and returned it to the old man got an anna from him. You could buy plates of biryani and sweet zarda rice with one anna from the food stalls by the steps of the Jama Masjid.

As they stood there, faces raised to the sky, Bulle Khan's red-and-black kite came swooping across like a dangerous tiger and went dipping towards the nawab's white-and-gold one. Then the strings of the two kites got all tangled up in battle and soon the nawab's white-and-gold lost, and the boys ran to catch it as it floated down lazily from the sky. Mushir could already taste the biryani.

Racing the other boys, with eyes on the kite, they sprinted through the lane, avoiding people, rickshaws, carts and wandering cows, and they caught the kite before it had even touched the ground.

Abbas grinned triumphantly at Mushir. 'Biryani!'

At their knocking on the nawab's haveli gate, a small side door opened slowly and Bakhtiar Khan's old personal servant, Fakru Miyan, peered out at them and asked suspiciously, 'Got the kite?'

'Got the annas?' Abbas shot back cheekily.

The boys were surprised when Fakru opened the gate and waved them in. They had never entered the haveli before. Fakru always paid them at the gate and shooed them away.

'Why, Fakru bhai?' Abbas asked nervously. 'What's the matter?'

Fakru gave a sad shake of his white-haired head. 'From today, after this kite was *also* cut, Nawabsaab has decided not to fly kites any more. So he doesn't want the kite back.' And with a long, gusty sigh, he said, 'That man gets crazier by the day . . .' and let out one more sigh.

'How can that be!' the boys exclaimed. 'Nawabsaab can't give up kites! What happened?'

'It is true.' Fakru nodded sadly again. 'It is impossible . . . just impossible . . . Without kites to distract him, his temper will get worse; he will trouble the servants all the time; and he will fight with everyone. Even Begum Sahiba is worried. Without kites to keep him busy, he will make our lives hell!'

Just then, they heard a voice yell from inside the haveli, 'Fakru! Where's that *namak-haram*? Fakru!'

'Here he comes . . .' Fakru looked very tired.

Nawab Bakhtiar Khan came stumping out into the courtyard, waving his walking stick. He glared at the boys. 'What are these boys doing here?'

'They came to return the kite, *huzoor*.'

'Haven't you told them I've stopped flying kites from today? What's the point when that badmash Bulle Khan keeps cutting them?'

Abbas spoke up. 'You need good thread.'

Nawabsaab stared at him.

'We need to make the *manja* properly, huzoor,' Mushir joined in. 'It is the manja that makes the difference.'

'Of course, I know that!' Nawabsaab glared at them and then turned to Fakru. 'Last time you said that the manja was made in Lucknow, and look! Bulle Khan has been cutting my kite every evening for a week!' He pointed to the kite that Mushir was holding.

Mushir gulped. All the biryani was going up in smoke, and he had to do something quickly. 'Huzoor, the best manja is made right here in Ballimaran. We can make it at home.'

'Hah! Fakru makes it at home, and his manja doesn't last a minute against that Bulle Khan's red-and-black kite.'

'We know how to make it, huzoor!' Abbas was now wheedling like a salesman. 'Everyone knows that Mushir and I make the finest, sharpest manja in Ballimaran, and we even sell it to Islamuddin the kite-wallah at Fatehpuri.'

Bakhtiar Khan looked thoughtfully at the boys as Fakru joined in. 'I am too old for manja-making. It needs a lot of energy, and these two will know what to do.'

'Give us a chance, huzoor.'

'It's our special, secret glue masala, huzoor!'

Bakhtiar Khan nodded. '*Theek hai!* Start work tomorrow. How long will it take to make one roll of kite thread?'

'If it is sunny, one day for the manja masala to dry properly,' Mushir replied promptly as an experienced manja-maker.

'Remember,' said Bakhtiar Khan, taking the kite from Mushir and waving at Fakru to give them an anna each, 'my kite Jahanbaaz is made with the best paper and bamboo from Murshidabad and cost me fifty *rupaiya*. If I can cut that Bulle Khan's red-and-black even once, I'll give you boys a gold mohur each.'

'A GOLD MOHUR!' Abbas and Mushir stared at each other in astonishment. That was a *lot* of money. They had never even seen a gold mohur in their life!

Later, munching the hot biryani—the rice fragrant with spices and full of tender meat—Mushir and Abbas dreamt of what they would do with the mohurs. Abbas just couldn't make up his mind. Would he take his family out for a meal to one of the big food shops in Gali Kababiyan and then buy lots of sweets? Or should he hire a tonga and go to the mela at Dilli Gate? But Mushir knew exactly what he wanted to buy with his mohur—a sherwani, a cap and shoes for his Abbu to wear at the mushaira.

Early next morning, Mushir and Abbas skipped their classes at the madrasa and got to work at the Nawab's haveli. In the haveli's courtyard, two slabs of wood had been fixed to the ground, where Fakru usually made the manja. Next to them was a grinding stone for smashing up the glass for the masala. The boys took a spool of the best cotton thread and ran it around the stakes. For the manja to be really strong, it would need at least eight layers of the masala on the thread. And to make the masala with which they would coat the thread, they pounded glass on the grinding stone into a fine powder and then combined it with a mixture of gum and flour to make a ball of very prickly dough.

This glass-filled dough had to be handled very carefully or it would cut their fingers. So they took long strips of cloth and wound them around their fingers like bandages. Then, carefully holding the masala, they rubbed it along the length of the thread, the gum making it stick. It was hot and sweaty work, as they went running back and forth, back and forth, between the stakes. After one coat of masala had dried, they would add another layer. Luckily, the monsoon clouds were nowhere to be seen and it was a nice sunny day.

In the evening, after testing the manja gingerly, Abbas said, 'It is ready.'

Mushir wasn't so sure. 'I think it needs one more coat of masala. It's not rough enough, and we know Bulle Khan uses really sharp manja.'

'Theek hai.' Abbas nodded. 'Let's test it. We'll wind some on a *chakri* and fly a kite with it now.'

As they climbed to the roof of Mushir's house, they saw that the sky was full of kites in all the colours of the rainbow. From here they flew their kite with the new manja, and as it battled and cut a few kites, Abbas got more and more confident. Then, from across the sky, Bulle Khan's red-and-black came swooping and swerving towards them like a dangerous eagle.

'Let's fight it!' Abbas yelled confidently. 'Cut it, Mushir!'

In the sky, the two kites got entangled. There was a sharp tug and, as they watched in horror, their kite floated downward and the manja hung loose in Mushir's hand.

'I told you the manja needed at least one more layer of masala!' Mushir said angrily.

Abbas nodded. 'We'll do it tomorrow morning.'

Rolling the manja around the chakri, Mushir thought desperately, *The mushaira is only a week away. I must get that mohur tomorrow, I must.*

The next evening, Nawab Bakhtiar Khan stood on the highest terrace of his haveli with Fakru, Mushir and Abbas standing behind him anxiously. Watching the white-and-gold Jahanbaaz rise slowly in the sky, Mushir had never felt so nervous in his life. The kite caught a gust of breeze and soared higher, swooping and dipping against the deep-blue monsoon sky, its gold tail catching the last rays of the sun.

Then from the right, Bulle Khan's red-and-black kite came rushing across the sky like a dangerous snake, and Mushir felt his heart thud even harder. 'Oh, Allah!' he prayed. 'Please help us. This is for a sherwani for Abbu!'

The nawab was muttering under his breath, 'I'll see you, Bulle Khan. Just you wait!' And he dipped his kite across the path of the red-and-black. The battle had begun. With their manja entangled, the kites rose higher and higher and, with a murmured oath, Nawabsaab gave a sharp tug on the manja.

As they watched with growing delight, the red-and-black kite suddenly sank and, with its manja cut, began to drift sadly towards the ground.

'Allahu Akbar!' yelled Bakhtiar Khan in triumph, doing a one-legged jig, as Fakru stood grinning and the boys yelled, jumped and hugged each other. Then Fakru pulled out two gold mohurs from his pocket and gave one each to the boys.

Nawab Bakhtiar Khan stood flying his kite, and Jahanbaaz flew free and unchallenged—the champion of the skies. Holding his mohur, Mushir stood there dreaming. One day, when his Abbu became a famous

poet, he would say, 'It is all because my son, Mushir, bought me this lucky sherwani.'

And Jahanbaaz, now the king of kites, soared too, just like Mushir's dreams.

Historical Note

When Bahadur Shah Zafar, the last Mughal king, was ruling from Delhi, there were many rich nawabs living in Chandni Chowk. They were lovers of poetry, painting, music, good food and had interesting hobbies like training pigeons and flying kites. The nawabs would compete with each other by trying to get one another's pigeons to come to their own pigeon coops and also by cutting the strings of each other's kites!

THEY CALL ME RAMTANU

His grandma had said to Parvez, 'You must visit Sheikh sahib's dargah tomorrow. The best time to go is at dawn as it is quiet and empty then, and you can say your prayers in peace.'

'*Ji*, Nani,' said Parvez obediently.

'And remember to chew some of the leaves of the imli tree,' his grandfather had reminded him. 'It will improve your voice.'

'*Ji*, Nana, I will,' said Parvez.

Parvez had had no intention of obeying them, of course. Imagine facing the torture of crawling out from under a warm quilt on an icy winter dawn to visit a dargah! It was out of the question. So Parvez simply strolled into the shrine in the evening, just before the sun began to set.

Also, he had no intention of chewing tamarind leaves like an idiotic goat either. He was interested in growing tall and building his muscles, not his vocal chords, and, as far as he knew, he needed to chew meat and fish cooked in ghee and drink lots of creamy milk to achieve that.

Parvez was in a very disobedient mood. His grandparents did not know it yet but he had actually left his home in Agra forever.

A week before, Parvez was loitering in their lane in Agra one afternoon when he saw Bhawani Chacha loading his bullock cart with sacks of spices and dals. Chacha was a travelling trader and supplied food items to nearby towns and villages, and he was always happy to take passengers in his cart.

'Where are you going this time, Chacha?' Parvez asked.

'Gwalior. I have a big order of red chillies from Jaipur, and coriander and mustard seeds from Panipat.'

'Gwalior! Oh, my nana and nani live there!' Parvez's ears perked up as his brain raced with a madcap idea. 'Chacha, can I come with you?'

Perched on a sack of coriander seeds, Chacha looked down at Parvez's eager face. 'Who will you go with?'

'Oh, I'll go alone!' Parvez waved a casual hand in the air.

'Alone? You are twelve years old, *beta*. You can't travel alone. We'll take five days to reach Gwalior ...' Then looking at Parvez's disappointed face, he added, 'Fine. I'll take you if you get your abbu to agree, and it will cost you money.'

The next morning, as always, his ammi put a freezing cold hand on his cheek and said gently, 'Time to get up, Parvez.'

'A little later ...' he pleaded sleepily.

'Your abbu is already in the *riyaz* room ...'

'Ohh ...' Parvez dragged himself from under the quilt and, shivering away, went to wash his face, brush his teeth and drink a glass of milk. His abbu did not like to wait during riyaz, and if Parvez was afraid of anyone in the world, it was his abbu.

His father was Ustad Amanullah Khan, the great *dhrupad* singer. Theirs was a famous musical family that traced their lineage to Miyan Tansen, the legendary singer who was the royal musician in the court of the Mughal emperor Akbar. So they belonged to the Agra gharana of Tansen, and every boy in the family was trained to sing classical music and carry on this great tradition. No one asked you if you wanted to sing or not. You just *had* to. Being a singer meant hours of daily practice called riyaz and, by his abbu's orders, his riyaz began at dawn.

Parvez had a musical voice and he loved singing; so that was not the problem. But he just *hated* riyaz—having to get up at dawn in the winter and then keep on singing till it was time to go to the madrasa to study. The rest of Parvez's morning was spent in reading, writing and arithmetic. When he got home, it was lunchtime, and by then he was so tired that he usually fell asleep. Then in the evening, when all his friends would be out in the lane, playing marbles and *gilli-danda*, he sat and went 'Sa . . . re . . . ga . . . ma . . .' once again.

Riyaz and study, riyaz and study—that's all he did every day. Was this a way for a boy to live?

Only on Fridays, when his abbu went to the mosque for his namaz, or when he was travelling for a concert out of town, did Parvez get any time to play with his friends. Even his ammi thought the morning riyaz was enough for a boy and that Parvez should be allowed to play in the evenings, but his abbu would not listen. Abbu said that even his father, Parvez's dadaji—another 'great' singer—had taught like this. *Just because Dadaji tortured Abbu,* Parvez thought rebelliously, *it does not mean Abbu should do the same to me!*

And that was why Parvez had persuaded his parents to let him visit Gwalior. His nana was a kind and understanding grandfather, and his nani never woke him up at dawn. He'd decided he was going to stay in Gwalior and never go back to Agra ever again.

Bhawani Chacha had said that the fare to Gwalior was going to be two rupaiya, that is sixteen annas multiplied by two ... and that was a *lot* of money. Parvez shook his *gullak*—the earthen pot in which he had been dropping paisas through the slit on top. It rattled sadly, and he knew he did not have more than a few paisas.

So that morning when Parvez entered the riyaz room, his brain was busy with one crazy plan after another to make Abbu give him two rupaiya for the fare. The room had a mattress covering the floor, on which many musical instruments were lying around—tanpuras, a *surbahar*, tablas, a pakhawaj. His abbu was sitting there, fiddling with the strings of a tanpura, and he said briefly, '*Sargam* ... start with that.'

Parvez picked up his small tanpura, ran his fingers across the strings—filling the room with the low droning tones—closed his eyes and began to sing the basic notes. Soon he was joining his father in singing one of his favourite *raag*s, Miyan ki Malhar. It had a soft, deep mix of notes that made him think of cloudy skies, the call of birds and the light patter of raindrops falling on dry earth.

After a while, the singing had warmed him up and the world had shrunk to just their voices and the drone of the tanpuras. As they wove the notes in an intricate melody, Parvez marvelled at how his father could pluck a strain out of thin air, improvising as

99

he sang. Parvez tried his best to repeat the notes, but sometimes the melody was so complicated that he gave up with a sigh and that made his abbu smile.

'That bit—' Parvez sang a few notes. 'That I'm not getting right . . .'

'One day you will. You are still learning . . . you sang well today.'

His father was pleased with his singing today; he usually wasn't on the mornings Parvez did not sing well. So he decided to try his luck at breakfast because soon after, his father's students would start arriving and he would not have the time to listen to Parvez.

As his ammi served hot parathas, a sabji of cauliflower and peas and glasses of hot milk flavoured with saffron, Parvez began, 'I met Bhawani Chacha yesterday and he is going to Gwalior soon . . .'

'So . . .?'

'Can I go to Gwalior with him and visit Nana–Nani?'

'Go alone?' His mother frowned.

'It'll cost money,' his father added.

'I'm twelve years old now. You let me go to the market alone,' he told his ammi. 'And it will only cost two rupaiya,' he said to his abbu. 'You got a bag full of silver rupaiya from that Nawabsaab last week. You are rich!'

'He needs a holiday,' Ammi said. To his surprise, his ammi was supporting him! 'All he does is riyaz and study ... a boy needs to play too. I feel so sorry for him having to wake up that early on cold mornings.'

'My abbu did the same—' his father began.

'Did you like it?' Parvez interrupted curiously.

'Er, no . . .' his abbu had to admit. 'I used to cry.' And then looking at his wife's and son's amused faces, he knew he had lost the argument. 'Fine, you can go.'

'Let him stay in Gwalior for a month and then we can go and bring him back.' His ammi looked very happy. 'Then I can spend some time with my parents too.'

So that was how Parvez came to Gwalior. But what no one in the family knew was that he had no intention of going back to Agra. Morning riyaz? Never ever again. Those days were over.

A week later, wandering around in Gwalior, Parvez walked into a mausoleum—the dargah of the Sufi saint Sheikh Muhammad Ghaus. This was a very important shrine for Parvez's family because one of the disciples of Ghaus was the singer Tansen and, as he had been told a thousand times, Tansen was his ancestor. So he had to be a singer and suffer all the pain and tears of early morning riyaz for *this* man who died centuries ago.

Usually when the family came to the dargah, his father would first pray at Ghaus's *mazhaar*, or grave, and only then would he enter the open pillared pavilion where Tansen was buried. There, his abbu would lie flat on the ground in worship for a long time. Now Parvez entered the pavilion, went down on his knees and touched his forehead to the floor like he had seen his father do.

'Miyan Tansen huzoor,' he whispered politely, 'my prayers to you. But I have come to say goodbye, O Great Singer! Even though I am your descendent, I have decided not to become a singer. So, *khuda haafiz*!'

As he whispered, Parvez felt a small shiver run along the marble floor and a soft breeze played through his hair. He looked around, but found he was alone. So he bowed again and then calmly left the gravesite.

The sun was setting, and the keeper of the dargah came with lamps—candles flickering under glass shades—and placed them around the mazhaar. The visitors were leaving, but Parvez decided to stay for a while longer. There was something about the silent air, the call of birds heading for their nests, the soft rustle of leaves, the fragrance of flowers and the smoking incense that made him feel oddly happy.

He went and perched on a corner of the veranda, leaning against a pillar, and looked around dreamily. 'You live in a good place, Miyanji,' he said to his ancestor. *This would be a great place for a concert*, he thought absently and then remembered that, just a few minutes ago, he had officially said goodbye to music. To his surprise, it did not make him happy at all.

Then he recalled that for two days he had done no riyaz at all. No one had dragged him out of bed; no one had glared at him when he made a mistake in his singing; no one had made him sing a line again and again. Instead, he had played marbles all morning and won a fantastic blue starry one. Life was good, he thought firmly, when he wasn't singing.

'I hear you are saying goodbye to music? What's happened to make you so angry?' a deep, mellow voice spoke behind him.

Parvez turned to look up at a man staring down at him with a curious smile.

'Giving up music when you can sing . . .' The man sat down beside him. 'What a stupid thing to do.'

Parvez sat up in protest. 'How do *you* know I am giving up music?'

'You just said so, there . . .' The man gestured towards the grave. 'To Miyan Tansen.'

Parvez frowned. 'How did you hear me? I whispered very softly.'

'I have very good hearing.'

'And why do *you* care?'

The man was silent for a moment, as if Parvez's question had surprised him. Parvez now got a good look at the man. He was quite old and his long grey

hair was tucked into a white turban. He wore a simple white *angrakha* and loose pyjamas, like Parvez's nana did, and a silver necklace as well as a thick bangle around his right wrist. The high-cheekboned face had a droopy moustache under a thick nose, large eyes under arched eyebrows and the forehead was lined. There was something oddly familiar about his face ... as if Parvez had met him before.

'Have we met before, huzoor?' he asked politely.

The man gave a short bark of a laugh, the teeth gleaming in the growing dark. 'I don't think so.'

'What is your name?' Parvez asked. 'And what do you do?'

'They call me Ramtanu, and I sing a little. And what is your name?'

'Parvez Khan, son of Amanullah Khan, the famous singer.'

'Ah! And does Amanullah Khan know his son is giving up music?'

Refusing to think about his abbu, Parvez quickly changed the subject. 'You didn't answer my question, Ramtanuji. Why do you care?'

'Because I don't understand you. Singers seek a good teacher and many never find one. You are fortunate enough to be a *shagird* to an ustad like your father, and you are walking away from a chance at living your life with music! Very few people can live doing what they love—sing, write, dance, paint . . .'

Ramtanu studied Parvez's mutinous face and smiled gently. 'What's the problem, beta?'

'No problem!' Parvez said shortly. This man was asking questions that made him very uncomfortable, and he was not going to reply.

'Are you not musical? You sing out of tune maybe?'

Parvez's eyes widened in protest. 'Of course not! I sing fine!'

Ramtanu's eyebrows shot up. 'So you *can* sing but you don't *like* singing. How extraordinary!'

'I *do* like singing.' Parvez found he could not lie to this strange man.

'Learnt any raags yet or is it still sargam?'

Parvez nodded. 'Raag Yaman . . .'

'Of course, all shagirds learn that first.'

'And I am starting Raag Todi, after which Abbu says he'll teach me Malhar.' Parvez gave a small smile. 'I like Malhar . . .'

Ramtanu's eyes sharpened at Parvez's approval of Raag Malhar. 'The second raag already! Not bad for a boy your age. How old are you?'

'Twelve and a half. And what do you mean it's not bad?'

'My guruji made me sing Yaman for two years . . .'

Parvez's eyes widened. 'Two years!'

'Until I could sing it in my sleep. The day Swami Haridas,' Ramtanu touched his right ear in respect at speaking the name of his teacher, 'began teaching me the second raag, I was so happy I felt like dancing!' His lips curved in a nostalgic smile. 'He was a tough teacher. Is your father like that? Does he hit you if you make mistakes?'

Parvez was shocked. 'Never! Your guruji *hit* you?'

'If my mind wandered, or if I sang a note wrong, or lost the rhythm . . . a quick slap, and it hurt.'

Parvez thought back to his riyaz time with his father and shook his head. 'Abbu glares at me if I make a mistake or if I yawn . . .' He mimicked his father's wide-eyed glare, making Ramtanu laugh. 'But he never hits me.'

'Hmm . . . Parvez, sing a little Raag Todi for me. I'm very fond of that raag.'

Parvez usually did not sing for strangers, but he did not know what made him obey Ramtanu. He cleared his throat, softly hummed the words of the *bandish* and then, closing his eyes and imagining his abbu listening to him, began to sing. As his high, clear voice rose in the still evening air, Ramtanu gave a small nod of approval. When he brought the melody to a close, Parvez opened his eyes and realized that some of the visitors at the dargah were standing around and listening to him. They all exclaimed 'Wah! Wah!' in praise, and it made him rather happy.

'What did you think?' Parvez inquired.

'Quite good for a boy who only knows two raags,' replied Ramtanu, 'but your *gayaki*—the melody that you weave around the words of the bandish—needs more work.'

'Abbu says the same. He says I hurry through. I have to learn to pause, think of the notes of the raag and play with them.' Parvez gave a puzzled shake of his head. '*Play?* How do I do that?'

'You'll learn. The basic notes of the raag are for you to use and create new melodies from. The more you sing, the easier it will be for you to improvise and create your own melodies. It just needs riyaz.'

Parvez nodded. He somehow understood. 'Sometimes when I am alone I can do that—play around—but I'm too scared to do it before Abbu ...'

'Never be afraid of singing what is in your heart. You'll find that your abbu will like it, and he'll correct you if you make a mistake.'

By this time all the people had left, the dargah compound was empty and quiet, the candles were guttering under the shades.

'You'd better go home, it's getting dark,' Ramtanu said.

Parvez felt a bit sad. 'Can I see you again?'

'I am here at sunrise and sunset.'

'How will I find you?'

'I stay here,' Ramtanu waved at the mazhaar of Muhammad Ghaus, 'next to my pir sahib. Why don't you come tomorrow?'

'I'll try.' Parvez began to walk away. 'I don't like getting up early . . .'

'The birds sing at dawn . . . the peacocks dance among the grass . . .' Ramtanu strolled along beside him. 'And maybe I'll sing for you.'

'I'll think about it.' Parvez nodded.

'You do that. I'll be here.'

Just then, Parvez saw his nana hurrying towards him. 'Oh, there you are! I was worried that you got lost! What were you doing here for so long?'

'I was talking to—' Parvez turned and found that the man called Ramtanu had vanished.

The next morning, no one had to drag Parvez out of bed. This had never ever happened before! He got up on his own at dawn and splashed water on his face and put on fresh clothes. His nani was in the courtyard, lighting the chullah and filling the quadrangle with smoke. She said in surprise, 'You are up early! Are you feeling well?'

'I am fine!' Parvez grabbed a dry roti and a raw carrot from the kitchen and, munching away, whizzed out. 'I'll be back soon. I'm going to the dargah.'

'Mad. Just like his father,' his nani muttered, coughing, all wreathed in the chullah smoke.

As he ran inside the dargah, Parvez saw Ramtanu's broad back in the distance. He sat cross-legged at the edge of the veranda, staring ahead. Past a patch of garden the land sloped down, and far towards the horizon the sun was barely visible behind the waves of mist floating through the still air. A dove called from the tamarind tree and Parvez remembered that he had refused to chew the imli leaves, even though his nana had ordered him to do so.

As he came closer, he realized that Ramtanu was singing Raag Bhairavi, a morning raag to welcome the new day. Raag Bhairavi was the raag of dawn, and Parvez had heard his abbu sing it many times. He crept up silently, sat down behind Ramtanu and listened. His voice was much deeper than his abbu's and, as the notes rose and fell, Parvez experienced something that happened to him very rarely—images appeared behind his closed eyes.

He never knew how this happened, but sometimes when he closed his eyes and listened to his abbu singing a raag, he would see these flashes of images. He saw falling rain when he heard Raag Malhar; a sunset when he sang Raag Hansadhwani; a royal palace when it was Raag Darbari Kanada. Now he saw Ramtanu laying flowers at the feet of a goddess and praising her through song as the sun rose before him.

Ramtanu brought the raag to a close and then turned and looked at the rapt face of the boy. 'Hmm ... what did you think?'

'Oh ... it was ...' Parvez, at a loss for words, just shook his head in admiration. 'When you sang—' and he hummed a bit. 'That was so beautiful.'

Ramtanu's eyes sharpened with interest at the way in which Parvez correctly captured the melody. 'You could sing like that one day. But, of course, now that you are saying goodbye to music, I don't—'

'Maybe I can listen?' Parvez asked optimistically.

'I suppose you can.' Ramtanu studied the solemn face before him. 'And what do you want to do with your life?'

'I want to become a wrestler.'

Ramtanu froze in shock. 'A wrestler? Why?'

'There is an *akhara* next to the temple in our lane where I see the wrestlers every day!' Finally Parvez could tell someone about his plans. 'I hear that Kallu Pehalwan, the top wrestler, makes lots of money. And they get all dusty, rolling around in the earth of the akhara pit, and they have such fun while wrestling.'

'And singing is not fun?'

'Not when I have to do riyaz every day.'

'What's wrong with riyaz, Parvez? During riyaz you have to sing, and you like singing, don't you?'

Parvez nodded and finally the truth came out. 'I hate getting up early! Ammi wakes me up at dawn, when it is so cold. Then after breakfast, I go to the madrasa, and by lunch I am so tired that I fall asleep. Then in the evening, when all my friends are playing, I have to do riyaz again. That is all I do—riyaz, eat, study, sleep, riyaz . . .' He gave a gusty sigh. 'Tell me, Ramtanuji, is that a life?'

'Ah, no! I understand now . . . too much riyaz!'

'Ammi says that I should be allowed to play in the evenings, but Abbu doesn't listen. He says that is the way he was trained by my dadaji. And—' Parvez's voice rose in protest, 'he did admit that it made him cry!' He gave a small shrug. 'So I'm not going back to Agra, and I'm not going to be a singer.'

'You'll be a wrestler instead.' Ramtanu's voice shook a little, as if he was trying to suppress a laugh.

'Correct!'

Ramtanu reached out and pressed Parvez's thin arm. His touch was surprisingly light, like a feather. 'Look at your muscles—they are so small. So how do you think you'll get the muscles of a wrestler, *haan*? You'll have to exercise and practise. Go and ask the *pehalwan*, and he'll tell you he gets up at dawn to exercise and then he wrestles all day. Do you think that is easy?'

'Get up at dawn? Practise all day? Are you sure?' Parvez was horrified! 'They have riyaz too?'

'They do! If you want to learn something, you have to practise.' Ramtanu paused and seemed to think for a while and then said, 'Maybe you could talk to your nana–nani and your ammi, and then they can all talk to your abbu? About letting you play in the evenings till you are a bit older?'

'Maybe . . .' Parvez perked up a little. It wasn't a bad idea, as he knew that his abbu always listened to his nana and nani. Also, now that the plan of being a wrestler was not so attractive, maybe he'd better go back to being a singer?

The two of them sat in companionable silence for a while as the sun vanished behind the intense floating mist. It seemed as if they were the only people in the whole world, surrounded by moving walls of smoke. Even Ramtanu seemed to appear and disappear, but Parvez could hear him humming softly.

'Tell me something, Parvez,' Ramtanu asked. 'Why did you come to Tansen's mazhaar to say goodbye to music?'

'Because he is the real problem.' Parvez gave a glum shake of his head.

'Tansen? Problem? But he died years ago!'

'So what? He is my ancestor and we are of the Agra gharana and—'

'Oh really?' Ramtanu interrupted him. 'You are a descendent of my . . . one of Tansen's sons? Which one? Bilas Khan or Tanras?'

'No. His daughter, Saraswati.' Parvez looked closely at Ramtanu. 'You seem to know a lot about Miyan Tansen.'

'A bit, yes . . .' He smiled slightly.

'Then tell me something. He married Sheikh Muhammad Ghaus's daughter Husseini, right?' Ramtanu nodded. 'So he was a Muslim?'

The old man answered, 'He was born a Hindu but then he became a follower of the Sufi pir, and so he also began to pray to Allah.'

'Then why did he call his daughter Saraswati? She is a Hindu goddess.'

Ramtanu grinned. 'Ah, quite a puzzle! Saraswati is not just the goddess of learning, she is also the goddess of music and Tansen liked to pray to her.'

'He prayed to Allah *and* to Saraswati? What religion did he belong to? Was he Hindu or Muslim?'

'He was a musician, and that was his only religion.' Ramtanu leaned forward and Parvez got a whiff of flowers and incense. 'Tell me something, you heard me sing a dhrupad in Raag Bhairavi. Doesn't your abbu also sing that raag?'

'Yes.' Parvez nodded, starting to understand what the old man was driving at. '. . . And he loves to sing Raag Durga.'

'And he goes to the masjid and says his namaz?'

Parvez nodded again.

'So what does that make him? Hindu or Muslim?' asked Ramtanu.

'A singer.' Parvez finally understood.

Ramtanu's voice was oddly gentle. 'Parvez, when you sing and it goes well—the notes flow and your voice is full of power—how do you feel?'

'Happy.' Parvez realized there were tears in his eyes as he confessed, 'I was just angry with Abbu. I can never give up music! There is nothing like singing with him ... and one day, I want to sit behind him on stage, playing the tanpura and—'

'He'll beckon you, and you'll join him in singing a dhrupad, a khayal or a thumri ... a Raag Malhar to the rains, a Bhairavi to Shiva, a Basant to Holi ...'

'You sing them all?' Parvez was wide-eyed.

'I used to, a long time ago,' Ramtanu replied with a nostalgic smile. 'I loved to sing a dhrupad to my king.'

'Your king? But we don't have a king any more. It is the angrez who rule us now, and they have a queen called Rani Victoria, who lives in England.' Parvez shrugged, adding, 'She knows nothing about raags.'

They sat silently in the courtyard for a while. The mist was now getting deeper and Tansen's mazhaar seemed to be floating in space. Ramtanu was going out of focus, as if he were moving, and his voice was becoming faint, as if coming from far, far away.

'My king was the great Mughal badshah Jalal-ud-din Akbar, and I sang sitting on a small island built in the middle of a lotus pool—the Anup Talao—in the beautiful city that he had built, called Fatehpur Sikri.'

Parvez stiffened in shock. A few months ago, he had seen Anup Talao on a day trip to Fatehpur Sikri, and his abbu had told him that this was the seat of Miyan Tansen.

Ramtanu was going on, his voice beginning to fade. 'There I was, a village boy called Ramtanu Pandey, singing before the greatest king in the world. And he was so pleased, he gave me the title of Miyan and awarded me with gold mohurs.'

'Miyan Tansen!' Parvez whispered, his heart thudding. 'You are Miyan Tansen!' He looked around, frantically trying to find Ramtanu in the blinding mist.

'Never stop singing, Parvez. You have a very good voice . . .' The voice was now so faint, Parvez could barely hear it.

The birds had fallen silent as Parvez sat frozen in realization. Then slowly, the mist began to clear, there was a quick flash of sunlight in the east and, looking around, he realized he was all alone. 'Ramtanuji? Miyanji?' he called out tentatively, scanning the place. 'Where did you go?'

Then far, far away, there was the soft echo of song, and Parvez thought, *Ah! He is singing Miyan ki Todi! Miyan Tansen's own composition . . .*

Historical Note

Tansen was the most famous singer in the court of the Mughal emperor Jalal-ud-din Akbar. He was born in a poor Hindu family and named Ramtanu, and his first guru was Swami Haridas. He later became a devotee of the Sufi teacher Muhammad Ghaus and married Ghaus's daughter Husseini. Ramtanu soon became the singer in the court of Raja Ramchandra Baghela of Rewa and was bestowed the title of Tansen. When Akbar heard about him, he invited Tansen to Fatehpur Sikri. Akbar affectionately called him 'Miyan' and is said to have awarded him two lakh rupees once for a concert. The Agra gharana of Hindustani classical music traces its lineage to the children of Tansen.

NEW SHOES FOR NAWABSAAB

'Did he taste the korma last night?'

'Yes, he did, and he said that there was too much garam masala...'

'Arre! Last week he said that there was too little because I was stealing all the garam masala from the kitchen!'

'What did you expect?' Abbu laughed. 'This is our Nawabsaab. You'll never get it right. Never, Karim bhai!'

'If he ever praises my cooking, I'll probably die of shock.'

As the two men laughed, the whole kitchen joined in.

On chilly winter mornings, the kitchen is the warmest and the friendliest place in Nawabsaab's haveli. I love sitting in a corner with a bowl of steaming nahari soup and slices of sheermal or bakarkhwani, dipping the bread in the soup, blowing on it and then munching happily as I listen to the conversations. You can hear the best gossip here, all spicy and hot, flavoured by the smells of the masala and reverberating to the clanging beat of iron pots and brass ladles.

My Abbu often says that if we did not laugh at the madness of our Nawabsaab, we would all end up weeping.

Let me introduce myself. I am Nasir and my abbu is Aziz Khan. And we were in the kitchen of Nawab Mirza Baig's haveli in Hazratganj just then, in the beautiful city of Lucknow. Abbu was chatting with his best friend, Karim bhai—the nawab's *bawarchi*, a legendary chef. So for anyone to say that Karim bhai put too much or too little garam masala in a dish is completely absurd, but then our Nawabsaab is an absurd man.

Abbu is Nawabsaab's khansama, his chief steward, which means he supervises the running of the haveli and now that I am fourteen, I help him with his work. I am learning the job because one day I want to be a khansama too.

Nawabsaab's haveli is divided into two open courtyards with rooms around them. We work in the outer courtyard, where the men of the nawab's family live, while the maids work in the zenana, where the women stay. Nawabsaab has three wives, and my ammi is the personal maid to Nawabsaab's most senior wife, Begum Sahiba.

Between Abbu, Ammi and Karim bhai, the haveli is run well, and they stay because Begum Sahiba really takes care of them and sees to it that they are given good salaries. For all his fussy complaints, Nawabsaab and his family would be helpless without them, and Begum Sahiba knows that.

Every morning, Abbu and I carry trays of breakfast to the men's bedrooms, and the maids do the same for the women in the zenana. Once the family breakfast has been cleared off, we go to the kitchen and Karim bhai hands us the steaming bowls of nahari and slices of creamy bread. He always pops a big dollop of butter in my soup and gives me an extra piece of bread as he understands that in winter, hard-working boys like me feel very hungry.

That morning, as Abbu headed back to Nawabsaab's room, I followed behind, carrying two pairs of shoes that I had polished to a gleam. In his room, Nawabsaab was still pacing around in his nightclothes, absently humming a tune, and I knew exactly what he would say to us.

'Ah, Aziz! Now, what do I have to do today?'

'Huzoor, this morning you have to meet Seth Arjan Das about the land in the village that you want to sell.'

'Ah! Um ... yes ...' He hummed on, looking bored.

'Then Raja sahib is coming for a game of chess, and he will stay on for lunch. Karim bhai is making the pulao that Raja sahib likes.'

'Of course! Chess! Wonderful!' He brightened up immediately. 'So, Aziz, what do I wear for chess?'

Here we go, I thought with a silent sigh. Can you imagine wearing special clothes for playing chess? Yesterday it was clothes for strolling in the garden, and last week we had a long discussion about what to wear to fly pigeons! Abbu says that Nawabsaab is choosy and careful, but I think he is quite mad.

Nawab Mirza Baig is the fussiest man I have ever met. Nothing pleases him, especially when it comes to his clothes. He is always complaining about how the buttons of his achkan do not match or are the wrong shape. His pyjamas are too tight or too loose, or the length of the achkan is too short or too long. Fuss . . . fuss . . . complain . . . complain . . . That is all he does *all* day.

As he sat in a chair and watched with a critical frown, Abbu pulled out half a dozen sets of clothes—achkans, kurtas, sherwanis, loose pyjamas, Aligarhi pyjamas, tight churidars, embroidered, plain . . . and Nawabsaab brooded over the whole lot.

Abbu asked, 'The blue achkan and the grey churidar, huzoor?'

Nawabsaab shook his head. 'Don't think so. It is not a blue kind of day.'

Now *what* is a blue kind of day?!

'The green achkan, Aligarhi pyjamas and the pashmina shawl maybe?'

Nawabsaab sat and pondered silently, saying nothing, as I prayed it was a green kind of day.

Meanwhile, I pulled out some of his shoes and laid them in a row at his feet—*nagras* with curled tips, backless slippers with the top covered in pretty embroidery, sandals in soft leather, *mojris* and chappals. The row of shoes and slippers stood like soldiers waiting for orders to march as I stood wondering what would make Nawabsaab start fussing that morning.

'Ah, Nasir!' He turned towards me. 'Let's see what you have for me.'

'Huzoor, how about these sandals?'

He looked down with a frown and stayed silent, making me sigh impatiently. It looked like a shoe kind of morning to me.

'Huzoor?' I asked anxiously.

'Nasir, I don't have anything to wear!'

I stared at him in surprise. There were six pairs of shoes before him, and more in the cupboard . . . and he had nothing to wear!

'I need something unique, Nasir.'

'Unique?' My heart sank.

'Yes! Today I am in the mood to design new shoes!'

Abbu and I exchanged a worried glance. Last month, he had decided to design kurtas and by the end of it, the tailor was weeping with rage. Now a poor shoemaker was going to get the *'Lajawaab! Bemisaal!'* or 'Unique! One of a kind!' treatment. I was already feeling sorry for him.

'I'll wear the brocade slippers with the green achkan today, but by next week I want new shoes, Nasir. So get me the best shoemaker in the city.'

'Ji, huzoor.' I sighed, already feeling tired.

That afternoon, I wandered in the market in Aminabad, looking for a shoemaker named Kallu Miyan. According to Karim bhai, Kallu Miyan was the best shoemaker in Lucknow and also the most expensive. I knew that Nawabsaab liked expensive things because then he could show off to his friends.

I entered a shop and looked at the rows of shoes lined up on the shelves. An old man with a white beard, wearing a wool cap and chewing paan, sat hammering nails into the sole of a shoe.

'Is this Kallu Miyan's shop, huzoor?' I asked politely.

'Who's asking?' The old man, still hammering away, did not even raise his head.

'I'm coming from the haveli of Nawab Mirza Baig and—'

'I did not ask that.'

'Oh, quite! I am Nasir, assistant to the khansama.'

Finally, he looked up. 'Well, Nasir Ustad, what does your nawab want?'

'Shoes, what else? New! Unique! Latest fashion!'

'I get the message,' he said with a grim smile. 'Does he have money?'

'More than you can imagine.'

'Good!' He got up slowly, groaned and held his back, popped a paan into his mouth and said, 'Let's go, Chhotay Ustad.'

I liked the name Chhotay Ustad, or Little Ustad. That is what I am.

We walked along Lucknow's busy streets in complete silence. Maybe great shoe artists have to think a lot to design that unique pair of shoes. Kallu Miyan stopped once to spit paan juice against the wall of a kabab shop and coughed twice. Arriving at our haveli, I led Kallu Miyan towards the living room and, as we got closer, I could hear Nawabsaab complaining as usual.

'Aziz, the tobacco is not the right mix. There is too little *amburi*.'

'Huzoor, it is made exactly the same way as every day.'

'Hmm . . .' I heard the bubble and gargle of the hookah as Nawabsaab took a few puffs. 'Something is not right . . .'

'Fussy, is he?' Kallu muttered to me.

'Very,' I mumbled back.

'Huzoor,' I said, entering the *baithak* where Nawabsaab was reclining on the divan, leaning against a bolster and smoking his hookah, 'this is Kallu Miyan, the best shoemaker in the city.'

Kallu Miyan salaamed as Nawabsaab sat up, cleared his throat and ordered, 'Nasir, bring all my shoes!'

So I ran breathlessly in and out with loads of shoes, laying them on the floor until the baithak resembled a shoe store. Soon Nawabsaab was in full flow, but Kallu Miyan didn't say a word, sitting cross-legged on the carpet and staring thoughtfully at the shoes with an expressionless face.

'See that curved tip in the Rajasthani mojri? I want the tip to curve higher . . . then *this* style of embroidery, but not *that* design. Now, about the heel—'

Kallu finally spoke. 'You want a pair in black leather with gold embroidery on top; with a very long and narrow toe and a curving tip with a round tassel.'

'Correct! Exactly!' Nawabsaab looked happy, which was very unusual.

'Not a good idea.'

There was a small silence. Nawabsaab frowned at Kallu. He was clearly surprised that anyone could disagree with him. I held my breath, waiting for the explosion that was sure to follow.

'What did you say, Kallu Miyan?' asked Nawabsaab with an ominous frown.

'Such a shoe will not be a good shoe. I can suggest another design that will be fashionable and comfortable.'

Nawabsaab leaned forward and glared at Kallu Miyan. 'You mean you can't make it!'

'No. I can make it.'

'Then make it! Name your price!'

My heart began to thud in nervousness as the two men stared at each other like two wrestlers about to start a fight.

Kallu Miyan gave a resigned shrug. 'It's your feet and your money.'

'The price, Kallu Miyan!' Nawabsaab's cheeks were flushed red.

'Sixty rupaiya.'

'Done!'

I stared at them in shock. *Sixty rupaiya!* My abbu earns that much in six months! And for a pair of shoes! The world is a very strange place.

Kallu Miyan put a sheet of paper under Nawabsaab's foot and took his measurements. Getting up, he said that the shoes would be ready in a week. Then he bowed and left, and I realized that all through the encounter he had not smiled even once, not even when he had greeted Nawabsaab with a salaam. The shoemaking business is obviously a very serious thing.

Very soon, the whole haveli had heard about Nawabsaab's encounter with Kallu Miyan. It was the first time that anyone could remember someone actually arguing and disagreeing with Nawabsaab. The next day, Ammi came to me and said that Begum Sahiba wanted to see me.

'Why?' I asked nervously. 'What have I done?'

'Oh, nothing!' She laughed. 'She wants to hear the shoe story.'

We entered the zenana of the haveli, where the women live. I walked through the sunny courtyard, where all the girls of Nawabsaab's family were playing as the maids moved about cleaning, dusting and putting clothes out to dry. I don't come into this part of the house very often. The zenana is the women's world.

Ammi led me to the door of Begum Sahiba's room and then went inside to get her. A chick curtain was hung across the door and I had to speak to Begum Sahiba through it. She kept a very strict purdah and did not meet any men who did not belong to the family.

'Begum Sahiba!' I heard Ammi call out. 'Nasir is here.'

A shadow fell across the curtain as I felt my mistress study me through the narrow chick slats. 'I hear, beta, that you take care of Nawabsaab's shoes?'

'Ji. I do.'

'How many pairs does he have?'

'Twenty-four pairs, huzoor.'

'Hai, Allah! And now he has ordered another for sixty rupaiya?'

'Ji.' I nodded.

'What will this shoe look like?'

'It is going to be black leather with gold embroidery on top, narrow toes, curving tip with a round tassel at the end.'

There was a small silence.

'Is that a shoe or a piece of jewellery for a dancer? The man is mad!' the voice across the curtain muttered worriedly. 'One day it was buying pigeons for two hundred rupaiya, then it was that horse he never rides—and now this! He will bankrupt us one day.'

'Huzoor, I don't think more shoes will be ordered,' I said carefully.

'Why not? He doesn't like the shoemaker?'

I shook my head. 'No, the shoemaker does not like *him*.'

After I said that, we all burst out laughing. Begum Sahiba then told Ammi to give me a rupee because this was the funniest story she had heard in a long time, and Ammi gave me two eight-anna coins. *I like her*, I thought happily as I went back, jingling the coins in my pocket.

A week later, I was hovering at the gate when I saw Kallu Miyan coming towards the haveli, carrying a cloth bag.

I ran up to him. 'Are the shoes ready?'

'Of course, Chhotay Ustad,' he growled. 'Just as the foolish man wanted.'

In the baithak, Kallu Miyan knelt at Nawabsaab's feet and opened his bag. From it, he took out the most ridiculous-looking shoes I have ever seen.

The shoes were made of black leather and the top was covered in gold embroidery so shiny they dazzled my eyes. The toe was so long and narrow that it looked like the snout of a crocodile, and then it rounded inwards in a huge curve and at the tip hung a bright, round gold tassel.

With a grim face, Kallu Miyan laid the shoes before Nawabsaab, who looked on, his brows knitted in thought. He clearly did not know what to say about his own wonderful design. After a long silence, he mumbled a bit uncertainly, 'Mmm ... quite unusual ... very different ...'

'Long, pointed toe, curving tip, round tassel and gold embroidery.' Kallu Miyan waved a hand disdainfully. 'Exactly as you had ordered.' He then proceeded to help Nawabsaab put on the new shoes.

Nawabsaab walked around the room, head bent, studying his feet.

It was an amazing sight! It looked like Nawabsaab was wearing two golden elephants on his feet, that had their trunks raised. As he walked, the tassels jiggled about like apples hanging from a tree. They swayed and danced on his feet, and then suddenly, because of the long, pointed toe, he tripped on the edge of the carpet and nearly fell flat on his face!

Abbu, who had been standing in the corner, watching the show, was grinning. I was biting my cheeks to stop myself from giggling, but Kallu Miyan's face was as solemn as ever.

'Um, Kallu,' began Nawabsaab, 'isn't the curling tip too high and, um . . . I think the toe is too long.'

'*You* gave the measurements.'

'I am a nawab, not a shoemaker!' He tried to sound very royal and disapproving. 'And my feet are hurting too.'

'I told you that day that you have broad feet and the toe is too narrow, but you would not listen . . .'

The two men were once again glaring at each other like two wrestlers.

'I know I told you!' yelled Nawabsaab, springing to his feet in a rage. 'But you could have—'

'You asked me to make it exactly the way *you* wanted! You said I couldn't make it! I could!'

Nawabsaab sat down and kicked off his shoes. He looked down at Kallu Miyan sitting cross-legged at his feet. The two men stared at each other for a long time, but Kallu Miyan did not blink.

'Theek hai!' Nawabsaab said finally. 'You win! Take these shoes back and make me a new pair . . .' he took a quick breath '. . . in your own design.'

'But you'll have to pay for this one,' said Kallu Miyan.

'Aziz, pay him.' Nawabsaab waved a royal hand, and Abbu handed Kallu Miyan a small bag of coins.

Kallu Miyan pocketed his payment and then, reaching inside his bag, took out a second pair of shoes! Everyone was stunned by this beautifully made pair. This one was made in soft black velvet with small silver stars embroidered on top and a broad, rounded toe. He slipped them on Nawabsaab's feet and said gently, 'Now, huzoor, try these.'

Nawabsaab, now quiet, wriggled his toes. 'They are soft . . . and light . . . and very comfortable!' He raised a leg and stared at his newly shod foot. 'They look very good too—and the stars are perfect.' Then he looked down at Kallu Miyan. 'How did you know I would like them?'

Kallu Miyan, busy putting the elephant shoes back in his bag, said calmly, 'I am the best. I *always* know.'

'Thank you, Kallu Miyan. Now, quote your price!'

'They are my gift to you, huzoor.' And for the first time, I saw Kallu Miyan smile. 'A pair of my best shoes for my fashionable Nawabsaab.'

I have to go and warn Begum Sahiba, I thought. It looked like more shoes were going to be ordered soon.

Historical Note

In the eighteenth century, the kingdom of Awadh became very powerful and its capital, Lucknow, was a centre of culture. The nawabs of Lucknow were famous for living in great luxury in huge mansions called havelis. They also wore the finest clothes and jewellery—silk achkans with diamond buttons, pashmina shawls, fur caps and, of course, very fancy embroidered shoes.

GOODBYE, PASHA BEGUM!

I'm sure all this marble stuff is very historical and beautiful, but right now I'm hungry, thought Binny grimly. *Lunch was hours ago, and Shah Jahan on an empty stomach is definitely not my scene.*

The problem was that no one ever listened to Binny. The family was on holiday in Delhi and, as always, it was her baba, the amateur historian, who was deciding where they would go next. So in the last four days, they had overdosed on history.

They had trudged around the Qutub Minar, filled with tourists; Humayun's Tomb, smelling of bats; some crowded, dirty lanes leading to a tomb whose name she'd forgotten . . . and now the Red Fort . . . oof! Monuments are okay—but what about shopping for wrap-around skirts at Janpath? Chaat at Bengali Market? And a shopping mall . . . *Puhleeze?*

Binny felt like standing in the middle of this marble pavilion and yelling from the rafters, 'THIS IS MY HOLIDAY TOOO!' but she was 100 per cent sure that even then no one would listen. *This is what happens when you are the youngest in the family. They think fourteen-year-olds don't have any brains,* thought Binny, grumbling. But what was bugging her even more was how her ma and her older sister, Malini, were on Baba's side. Ma loved old buildings and was forever going off to visit museums, so it was understandable. But Malini? What was wrong with *her*?

Sometimes Binny got so sick of her angelic sister. Malini never did anything wrong, *ever*! She topped her class, sang Rabindra Sangeet looking all holy, and even painted! On the other hand, Binny had barely scraped through the last physics test and, according to Ma, wore jeans and tees that were too tight and always wasted her time watching cricket on TV. As for singing ... ah, well, let's *not* go there ...

'Come and look at this inlay work on the marble!' Baba beckoned them closer. 'See how they have created these flowers ...'

'Ooh ... that flower looks so real!' Malini breathed admiringly as she peered closely at a pillar.

'It took dozens of separate pieces of coloured stone to form a single flower ...' Ma recited. As always, she was reading from her travel guidebook.

Binny frowned at the droopy yellow-gold flower and said, 'The petals are exactly the colour of cheese … y'know, on top of a pizza?'

They all laughed but refused to take the hint. Family comedian, that's what she was.

After some time, they were out of the sun's glare and inside *another* pavilion, which Ma announced was called the Rang Mahal—the Palace of Colours. Binny looked around and couldn't see any colours anywhere. It was all the same—pale-cream, dirty-looking old marble.

I think hunger is making me dizzy, Binny thought gloomily as she dragged along behind the family, who were all marching ahead energetically. Her feet were aching, her eyes were tired and there was a funny thumping at the back of her head. *I think I'll rest a bit here and join them later.*

The small alcove at one end of the Rang Mahal was blessedly quiet and cool. Binny slid to the floor in a corner, leaned against the cool stone wall, stretched out her legs, her head dipping forward, and she was asleep.

A pungent, musky smell made her sneeze and Binny woke up with a heart-thudding start. As her eyes snapped open, she immediately realized that it was night. She was sitting in a room lit by candles, all the tourists had vanished and the family had forgotten about her.

'Candles? Oh, hell! Load-shedding!'

She scrambled up and looked around in panic. Candles in tall holders stood in the arched niches in the walls and, oddly, there were spots of dancing lights above her. She looked up and noticed tiny mirrors set in the ceiling that were reflecting the candle flames. 'A mirrored ceiling! That's a real cool way to light up a room,' murmured Binny. 'We should try it at home. Would save electricity too . . .'

Binny wandered out of the small room and into the main hall, and then stood petrified with shock. Her eyes wide, mouth open, heart galloping. Her feet were stuck to the floor and when she tried to speak, no sound came from her dry throat.

Everything had changed!

Just that afternoon, when she had stood right here, it was a bare room—just stone walls, pillars and ceiling. Now the floor was covered in soft Persian carpets woven in jewelled colours, and she could feel their silky softness under her bare feet. *Bare feet? Whaaa—?* She looked down at her toes, wriggling them, bewildered.

Where are my sneakers? she thought. And how could she have possibly changed her clothes? What was this really weird filmy sort of outfit? Binny panicked even more clutching at her dress, which was a short kurti with very loose sharara pyjamas and a thin, transparent chunni draped over her head. Clothes she would not wear if it killed her.

Binny began to look around, feeling more and more astonished. She wondered how and *when* the Rang Mahal had been turned into a Hindi film set so fast. There were low wooden divans and big round bolsters covered in satin strewn around on the carpet. The room glowed in the mellow golden light of candles and tall brass oil lamps, and silk curtains hung from the open archways.

Suddenly she noticed that there were only women around her. 'This was part of the Mughal harem...' Her mother's words—as she'd read from the guidebook—from earlier in the day came back to her. There were women in shimmering clothes that seemed to float around their bodies as they flitted past her; others sat at the windows, chatting; but somehow, their figures were oddly hazy, the edges forming and fading as if they had been shot through a camera that was out of focus. Binny stood paralysed. She heard a hum of conversation but could not understand what they were saying. It was as if someone was speaking somewhere far, far away.

A soft, burbling sound made her look down and her heart leapt with delight. Through the middle of the pavilion, a stream of water was flowing along a marble channel, and in the centre was a fountain carved in the shape of a blooming lotus. The bottom of the channel was decorated with flowers engraved in coloured stone, and they swayed and shimmered as if coming to life under the flowing water. Rose petals floated on the surface of the pool, filling the air with their delicate fragrance.

'Oooh! This is so awesome!' whispered Binny, kneeling beside the fountain. And when she sniffed, it was that smell again—heavy, musky and sort of cloying and headachy . . .

'What are you doing here, girl?' a high-pitched, scratchy voice spoke behind her, making Binny leap up and turn nervously. A short and stocky woman stood before her, her heavy-cheeked face fierce with rage. 'Get back to work!'

'Work?' Binny asked, puzzled. 'What work?'

'The work slave girls do, you idiot! Go dust my room.'

'*Slave* girl? You mad or what?' Binny's temper was up. 'I don't even dust my own room, lady, why should I dust yours?'

The stocky woman stared at her, at a loss for words—quite obviously, she was not used to people speaking to her like this. She wore a purple kurta and sharara covered with ghastly gold embroidery and was dripping with jewels—layers of diamonds around her short, thick neck and heavy earrings swinging by

her plump cheeks. Her hair was dyed a violent orange with henna and her small, beady eyes were smeared with kohl.

The woman recovered her voice and sneered. 'Do you know who you're talking to, girl? I'll make you pay for this!'

Binny blinked. Was she seeing things or was that smoke coming out in angry wisps from the woman's mouth? And the smoke seemed to be forming words in the air before floating away. She leaned forward, trying to read the fading script . . .

'Um . . . I can't read anything, man! Are you speaking in Urdu by any chance?'

'*Kya?*' The woman's mouth fell open.

'You must have been smoking a hookah or a cigarette or something, because the smoke is turning into words.'

'*Besharam ladki!*' the woman hissed and suddenly reached out to grab Binny's left earlobe, in the process digging her long nails into Binny's neck. As Binny squirmed, trying to free herself, the woman's angry, unpleasant face came closer and closer, and Binny smelled her breath and gagged. It was like getting a lungful of fumes from an open sewer, a mix of mysterious rotting things.

The face was an inch away from her and Binny stared into eyes that were red with rage, and when the woman spoke, her yellowed teeth seemed to become long and pointy, like the fangs of a snake. Binny twisted her head free from that icy hand and quickly stepped away.

'God! Your breath smells *awful*! Don't you ever brush your teeth?'

'That's enough!' the woman muttered through gritted teeth and clapped her hands. *'Koi hai?'* And instantly two women ran up and stood bowing before her. 'Bring this girl to my apartment, she has to be punished.'

'Ji, Begum Sahiba.'

The maids caught Binny by her arms. 'Ow!' she protested. Their hands were so cold! It felt as if they had dunked them in ice water. And, like Begum Sahiba, they smelled unpleasant—a mix of rotten bananas and burning garbage. Binny sneezed again.

Protesting loudly, she was dragged back to the room in which she had fallen asleep. Now it was well lit by lamps, and Binny was made to stand before Begum Sahiba, who lolled on a silk cushioned seat, leaning against a fat bolster. A tray with a decanter of wine and glasses, as well as a hookah stood beside her and, noticing them, Binny of course had to say something.

'Do you know, Begum Sahiba,' she asked with a fierce, disapproving frown, 'that smoking tobacco can give you cancer?'

Ignoring her words, the plump Begum pointed a finger at her, talking in a sibilant whisper, 'You'll pay for this, you impertinent slave! Just you wait!' And, as Binny watched in horror, her finger seemed to grow longer and longer until it was touching Binny's chin. It was a slimy, icy-cold touch that made her jerk her face away, and immediately the finger moved away and the plump hand looked normal again.

At a wave from the begum, the maids tied Binny's hands with a strip of cloth and pushed her down until she was crouching at the begum's feet. Binny's heart sank as the begum, who was now drinking a large glass of wine, yelled at them to fetch the whip.

'This is kidnapping, lady,' Binny tried to sound brave. 'If I start screaming, my father will come and—'

The maids started laughing behind her in a nasty, sniggering way, and one of them told her that if her father tried to enter the *haramsara*, he would be immediately cut to pieces by the soldiers at the gate.

Binny swallowed and decided to change her tactics. 'Look, lady . . . Begum whatever . . . there has been a mistake. I'm Binny Chatterji and I live at B/51, Southern Avenue in Kolkata. I'm a stranger in this city, so if I have done anything to make you angry, I'm sorry, but . . .'

Begum Sahiba leaned forward with a menacing snarl and once again Binny was overwhelmed by that horrible smell. 'I don't care where you came from. No one gets away with insulting a princess of the Timuriya Dynasty . . . do you hear?'

If she's a princess, then I'm the President of India, thought Binny but wisely kept her mouth shut.

'I'm going to enjoy stripping the skin off your back, slave girl! Bring the whip here!'

Binny was now surrounded by Begum Sahiba and her maids, and she nearly fainted in panic. Their icy, slippery fingers were clutching her arms and their long nails dug into her skin. One of the maids brought her face close, and her long tongue flicked in and out of her mouth like a lizard's, as she whispered, 'I'm going to love watching you bleed . . . oooh!'

Binny kept on wriggling and protesting. What did they think? That she would get so scared that they could whip her for fun? Then a sudden thought flashed through her mind: *When I go back to Kolkata, I have to start martial arts classes.* Binny tried to lunge at the maids, kicking one in the shin. But the begum seemed unaffected; she sauntered over, swinging the whip in this scary, menacing way.

Binny had had enough. *'BACHAO!'* she yelled at the top of her voice.

A maid pushed up Binny's kurta, revealing her bare back, and the begum raised the whip.

'SAVE ME FROM THIS MAD WOMAN!' Binny's yells got even louder and then . . .

'Stop!' said a calm, firm voice. 'Let her go immediately!'

Her arm still raised, the begum froze and her face flushed with rage, and then, to her surprise, Binny found herself free. She stood up. She turned to her rescuer and sniffed . . . she could smell jasmine and sandalwood.

A tall, slim woman with large, gentle eyes and clad all in white stood at the door. 'What are you doing, Roshan? How many times have I told you that no one in the haramsara will be whipped?'

'This girl is impertinent, Appa . . .'

Binny stared in surprise as, before her eyes, Begum Sahiba seemed to shrink in size and looked sort of apologetic.

'If anyone is undisciplined, they are to be brought before me for judgement.' The lady in white spoke softly, but everyone seemed to obey her. 'I'm the head of the harem, you may remember . . .' She turned to the maids. 'Untie her hands.'

'Ji, Pasha Begum.' The maids bowed, and Binny's arms were free.

'You'll regret this, Jahan!' Begum Sahiba said fiercely.

'Thank you, ma'am!' Binny sighed in relief. 'You saved me! I'd hate to be whipped, you know!' Then she bowed slightly. 'My name is Binny.'

There was a flicker of a smile at the edges of the pale-pink lips. 'I'm very pleased to meet you, Binny. Follow me, child.'

Binny followed the figure in white out of the claustrophobic apartment and on to an open terrace. She took a deep, shaky breath of the fresh night air. The stone floor was cool under her feet. She looked up at the dark arc of the night sky strewn with sparkling stars. On her left, the terrace ended in a low screen railing and beyond it, she spotted a wide stream of water shimmering silver in the moonlight.

'How strange! That's River Jamuna,' she wondered aloud, 'and it is flowing right below the walls of the fort!' She vaguely remembered seeing a road and a park below the walls when she had peered out of an arched window of the *diwan-i-aam* in the morning while exploring the fort with her parents.

Once again Binny thought she was getting an attack of night blindness or something, because the pale figure seemed to be flitting ahead of her—fading away and coming into focus again. Sometimes she couldn't see Pasha Begum at all and had to follow her by sniffing that trail of flowers. It was a heady mix of jasmine, sandalwood and a hint of rose. *She is wearing attar*, Binny concluded, remembering a tiny vial of perfume on her ma's dressing table.

They entered another pavilion and then Binny followed the lady in white into a quiet room. Unlike the room of the plump lady, which was stuffed with divans, boxes and cushions, here there was just the welcoming expanse of a carpet and a few bolsters.

Binny noticed that the niches in the wall held books. Pasha Begum had to have been reading because a big bound volume was placed on an X-shaped wooden stand and a tall thick candle was beside it.

Binny bent to look at the open book and saw that on the left-hand page was a picture—a delicately coloured miniature painting. She also got a closer look at Pasha Begum's face in the light, and noticed the lines of laughter around the grey eyes and the lips that seemed always ready to curve in a smile.

'You like it?' Padshah Begum asked as Binny studied the painting of a domed building with trees all around. 'This is the dargah of the great Sufi saint Sheikh Nizamuddin Auliya ...'

'Nizamuddin! Right!' Binny suddenly remembered the tomb at the end of the narrow, dirty lanes. 'We went there yesterday, and a man was singing a lovely song.'

'It must have been a qawwali of the poet Amir Khusro. I often go there to pray at their graves. It is my favourite place. So you liked it too?'

'Oh yes!' breathed Binny. '... And later, that lunch of shami kababs and rumali rotis was like totally amazing!' She stopped to think. There was something else she had seen at Nizamuddin ... if only she could remember ...

'You're hungry.' Pasha Begum laughed and clapped her hands. Instantly there was a plate of shami kababs in front of Binny. 'Eat quickly, Binny, before they grow cold.'

They were the strangest kababs Binny had ever eaten, and the most delicious. They were soft, spicy and crunchy, but the moment she bit into one, it seemed to melt and vanish in her mouth. It was a bit like biting into candyfloss—just that it tasted like kababs.

Binny let out a soft burp of happiness and grinned at Pasha Begum. 'Thank you, that was perfect!' She continued, 'You arrived just in time, ma'am. I nearly got whipped by that fat lady.'

There was an amused gleam in the large eyes. 'That fat lady is my younger sister Roshan.'

'Oh, I'm sorry! I apologize!'

'You don't have to. I know she is a very bad-tempered woman. I heard her yelling for her whip and I had to stop her.'

'It's really lucky for everyone that you are the head of the harem,' said Binny. 'And she has to obey you, right?'

'Yes, and also because I'm older than her.'

'Well . . . um . . .' Binny leaned back comfortably against a bolster, feeling very at home in this serene room, and confessed, 'I don't always obey my older sister, Malini.'

Pasha Begum, who had been absently turning the pages of the book, looked up. 'You don't?'

'It's not easy being a younger sister, y'know. Malini is sort of perfect and angelic—a bit like you. Good at studies, can sing Rabindra Sangeet, and she even paints!'

'And you don't do any of those things?' The eyes were crinkling with amusement again. 'Aren't you good at anything?'

'I'm not bad at studies actually. Just that physics is not my hot subject, but then I really rock at sport— the long jump, the 100-metre sprint . . . *and* I'm in the school basketball team.'

Pasha Begum looked rather confused. 'You like to jump and run, that I can understand. But *basket*? You play with baskets? And physics—what is that?'

'Um . . .' Binny tried to imagine explaining the rules of basketball to this old-fashioned lady and said quickly, 'Physics is a subject we study in school, and basketball, um . . . well . . . it's just a game.'

'So you think Roshan has a tough time because of me?'

'Well, the thing is no one takes you seriously if you are the youngest, and maybe that's what's made her so bad-tempered. You are also so beautiful and people listen to you, and I'm sure she's not very popular either . . .'

Pasha Begum laughed. Even her laughter was musical. 'I had never thought like that before! Maybe I should be more patient with her from now on. You see,

I was staying in Agra with my father and Roshan was made the head of the haramsara by my brother, who is the king. Then our father died, and the badshah brought me back to Delhi and made me the head again. Roshan was not pleased.'

'I really think she shouldn't smoke or drink so much wine,' Binny said thoughtfully. 'It makes her smell a bit.'

'I'll give her the message. I'm sure she'll be very pleased to hear it.' Pasha Begum gave her a wide-eyed, solemn look that made Binny grin.

'You're cool, Pasha Begum. Really cool.'

'I suppose that's a compliment, so thank you. You are a strange girl, do you know that?' Pasha Begum went back to reading her book and then rubbed her eyes. 'I'm growing old, Binny. Reading by candlelight makes my eyes ache and the words begin to blur.'

'You need reading glasses.'

'I need rose water.'

She reached towards a silver bowl of water with rose petals floating on top. She dipped her elegant long, pink-tipped fingers into it and then pressed them to her eyes. Binny blinked. Was she seeing right? The rose petals seemed to float in the air, a few inches above the swirling water in the bowl. She blinked once more and the petals were back in the water again.

'Do you write, Pasha Begum?'

'A little. Some poetry. Now I'm writing a book on the great Sufi saints of Hindustan. Do you like to read?'

'Both Malini and I read all the time. I love books about nature—animals, birds, flowers, trees...'

'Then you should write a book about flowers, and your sister can draw the pictures—of marigolds, roses, chameli, champa, lotus...'

'You smell of jasmine and roses,' Binny chipped in.

'My great-aunt Begum Nur Jahan and her mother created the attar of roses, and I mix that with the essence of jasmine and sandalwood to create my own perfume.' She stretched out her slim arm towards Binny, who bent her head to sniff deeply at her wrist. 'Like it?'

'Oh yes! I love it. It smells like spring.' Binny, feeling truly happy, could not stop herself and reached out to touch the wrist. It felt like she was touching a cloud...

She looked up and Pasha Begum had suddenly vanished. The carpet before her was sparkling with hundreds of stars—a shimmering spread of silver that faded slowly and then everything went dark before Binny's eyes.

Binny blinked and looked around, feeling confused. Where was she now? Where was Pasha Begum? She realized she was crouched in a corner of the room with the mirrors, but it was bare again—no carpets, curtains or furniture—and lit by sunlight pouring in through the windows.

Sun? Is the night over? Binny scrambled up. Suddenly, all she wanted was to find her family, and so she ran out to the terrace . . . and there she saw them! They were coming out of the museum, looking around anxiously, as if they were searching for her. Her heart singing with relief, Binny ran up to them, and her ma gave her a huge smile. 'Where did you go? I was starting to panic.'

'I sat there . . .' Binny pointed behind her, 'and rested a bit. My legs were aching.'

'And you're hungry.' Her baba put his arm around her shoulders. 'We'll have ice creams now, and *you'll* decide where we'll have dinner.'

'Well, I did have some Mughlai kababs . . .' Binny began to explain.

'Biryani and rogan josh then, a true Mughlai meal at Jama Masjid,' her father said firmly. 'And tomorrow, it's a day at Janpath.'

'Oh, good!' Malini gave a small jump of delight. 'I've had enough of history.'

They strolled down the arcaded bazaar called Chhatta Chowk towards the Red Fort's Lahori Gate, feeling tired but happy. Binny was walking with her father, her head still whirling a bit. She tucked her hand around his arm and asked, 'Baba, who was Pasha Begum?'

'Pasha or Padshah Begum was the title of Princess Jahanara, daughter of Shah Jahan, because she was the head of the Mughal harem.'

Binny remembered the plump lady in purple calling her Jahan. 'Her sister was Roshanara, right?'

'Correct. When their mother, Mumtaz Mahal, died, Jahanara was just seventeen. She was appointed the new head of the harem in her mother's place, and it was a tough job managing a harem of hundreds of women.'

'Then what happened?'

'When Shah Jahan fell ill, his four sons—Dara Shikoh, Shah Shuja, Murad Baksh and Aurangzeb— began to fight for the throne. Jahanara supported Dara, and Roshanara was on Aurangzeb's side. Aurangzeb killed Dara and Murad. Shuja ran away and was never heard of again. Then Aurangzeb imprisoned his old father in Agra Fort and—'

'Jahanara stayed with him,' Binny completed his sentence.

'Yes, for eight years.' He dropped a kiss on her head. 'Hey! You're getting interested in history!'

'What happened when Shah Jahan died?' Malini joined in.

'Aurangzeb went to Agra and brought Jahanara back to Delhi. He gave her a separate palace and made her the head of the harem again. During her father's reign, she was called Begum Sahib but now Aurangzeb gave her the new title of Pasha Begum, the Princess Royal.'

'So Jahanara forgave Aurangzeb?'

'Yes. You see, in a way Jahanara must have understood Aurangzeb's dilemma. In a Mughal battle for the throne, usually only one son lived to become king. So if Dara had been the victor, he would have executed Aurangzeb.'

'Brothers killing brothers!' Her ma shivered. 'What a bloodthirsty family, these Timurids.'

'I thought they were called the Mughals?' Malini asked.

'They preferred to call themselves Timuriya, as descendants of Persia's king Timur the Lame.'

Binny recalled Roshanara calling herself 'a princess of the Timuriya dynasty'. 'And what happened to Jahanara?' she inquired eagerly.

'She lived into her sixties, peacefully, reading her books, writing poetry, and she was famous for her charity. She was buried at—'

'Nizamuddin Dargah! She was buried near the tomb of her favourite saint!' Binny suddenly remembered everything. She thought of the marble grave in an open-screened enclosure. The grave only had earth on top, on which green grass and plants grew, because Jahanara wanted her grave to be open to the sky, the sun and rain—like the graves of the poor. Binny closed her eyes, thinking of the gentle, serene face.

'Goodbye, Pasha Begum!' she whispered as a pigeon cooed somewhere in the eaves and a soft breeze blew across her face like a gentle hand stroking her cheeks. Then, just for a magical moment, a swirling aroma of jasmine floated past, fragrantly enveloping her in a gentle farewell.

Historical Note

Jahanara Begum and Roshanara Begum were the daughters of the Mughal emperor Shah Jahan. They lived in the marble palaces of the Red Fort in Delhi. Jahanara, as the eldest daughter, was also the head of the Mughal harem and she had the title Padshah, or Pasha Begum in short. The two sisters had very different characters and did not get along. Roshanara Begum was not popular with the people, who all loved and respected Jahanara.

Soldiers, Badshahs
and Englishmen . . .

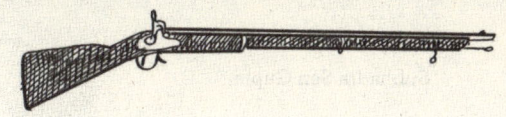

THE GORA PALTAN IS HERE!

The two boys were gathering melons by the Jamuna when the horsemen appeared on the opposite bank of the river. It was the early morning of a typical hot summer day in Delhi, the kind that ripens the watermelons and makes them fill up with sweet, cool juice.

Bishnu had tapped one melon to see if it was ripe and then said to his best friend, Sadiq, 'This one sounds good...'

Sadiq had bent down, about to cut the stem with his knife, when he'd heard the thudding sound of hooves. He'd looked up with a frown. 'What's that? Horses? So early in the morning?'

The boys stood and stared down the river, shading their eyes against the morning sun. In front of them was the bridge of boats that connected the opposite bank to the fortress of Salimgarh, and beyond that, near the horizon, they spotted a cloud of dust that grew larger and larger as it came closer to the river.

By then all the people who were bathing in the river were standing and staring as the rolling sound of hooves grew louder and louder.

'It sounds like thunder . . .' Sadiq said quietly, feeling oddly afraid.

'But whose horsemen are these? They look like soldiers,' Bishnu wondered aloud. 'Our badshah, Bahadur Shah, has no army.'

'It's the gora *paltan*!' Sadiq screwed up his eyes to see better and spotted that some of the horsemen were wearing the red jacket of the army of the East India Company.

'Sipahis! But why are they riding so fast?'

'Isn't that the road to Meerut?'

By then the soldiers had come to a sharp halt at the bridge of boats, the horses stamping their feet in impatience. This bridge had been made by tying together a row of boats with strong ropes. Then planks of wood had been laid over the boats to create a narrow floating bridge. People walked across easily, and even a bullock cart could cross over very slowly as the bridge bobbed up and down in the water.

'They can't come across all together with the horses!' Sadiq said worriedly. 'The bridge will sink.'

Then they saw one of the soldiers, who seemed to be the leader, wave and shout an order. The sepoys now began to ride very carefully over the bridge a few horsemen at a time. Some of the riders got off and led the horses across. Bishnu looked at the sepoys carefully and noticed that many of them were not in uniform. Some were carrying rolls of bedding and even cooking pots on their horses, and a few were riding two to a horse.

He remembered the Company Bahadur soldiers he had seen marching on the streets of Chandni Chowk: they were all perfectly dressed in red jackets, white trousers, high black boots and peaked white caps, and they always rode in neat rows—not in this helter-skelter manner. These men looked dusty and dishevelled, as if they had come from fighting a battle, and a few even had bandages around their arms and heads. Something about this loud, excited crowd made Bishnu very nervous.

He turned to Sadiq. 'I don't like this . . . let's go home.'

'What about the watermelons?'

'We'll pick them tomorrow.'

The boys headed back to Chandni Chowk. They walked along the red sandstone walls of the Laal Qila and then slipped through one of the side gates to walk down the road past Jama Masjid. They lived in a narrow gali that curved away from the broad street called Dariba with its silver and gold shops. Looking around the typical early morning scene, it was clear to the boys that no one had heard about the horsemen who had come riding down the Meerut road.

It was just another day on Dariba as they went hurrying towards home. The bullock carts creaked under sacks of grain and vegetables; a man got off a palanquin and began to argue about the fare with the two bearers; smoke rose from the chullahs being lit in kitchens; and a *bhishti* trotted past, carrying his leather sacks of water, which he would sell by the glass to thirsty people during the day.

By the time the two got home, Sadiq's father, who rode a tonga, had already left, but Bishnu's father, who sold vegetables, was picking up his baskets laden with potatoes, beans, spinach and gourd. Two baskets hung at the ends of a long bamboo pole that he now laid across his shoulders.

'Where are the watermelons?' he asked Bishnu, displeased. 'I was waiting for them. Why are you so late?'

Bishnu shrugged. *Why do fathers only ask you angry questions?* 'We didn't bring them. The gora paltan is coming, Bapu! We saw a huge army of horses coming down the Meerut road.'

'Gora paltan?' Bishnu's father stopped to listen to their report and then turned to leave. 'I'm sure you two are imagining things. Anyway, I'll find out what's happening soon enough. Someone will know in the bazaar.'

Sadiq and Bishnu had work to do in their homes. The cows had to be milked and the goats had to be fed. Soon Sadiq was sent off by his mother to buy some sugar from the market, while Bishnu helped his mother sweep the courtyard. The boys knew it would be close to noon before their mothers let them go and play. Usually around noon Bishnu would peer over the courtyard wall and yell, '*Saaadeeeq!* Let's go!' and they would run to join their friends in the street outside. They would play well into the evening and by this time Bishnu's father would be home, but Sadiq's father would return only when darkness fell.

However, Bishnu was sitting on a charpai in the courtyard, busy shelling peas, when he looked up in surprise to see his father come hurrying back home before noon, the baskets still half-filled with vegetables. He caught sight of his father's wide-eyed, sweaty face and knew that there was trouble.

'The sipahis have occupied the Laal Qila and our king has been forced to join them! They have killed some of the goras who were inside the fort!' his father shouted. 'This is war!'

Hearing the shouting and the noise, people had run out of their houses and crowded around Bishnu's father. They wanted to know everything that he had heard in the bazaar. So Bishnu's father told them: The sepoys of the British Army in Meerut had rebelled and killed their English officers and then ridden all night to arrive at the Red Fort the next morning. They had forced their way into the palace of Badshah Bahadur Shah Zafar and declared him their leader. They wanted the king to lead them in a fight to throw the East India Company out of Hindustan.

'Is the king willing to do that?' someone asked doubtfully. 'He is old ... and he is a poet, not a warrior.'

'I heard that his sons Mirza Mughal and Mirza Khizr Sultan want him to lead the sipahis,' Bishnu's father said, 'but he can't make up his mind.'

'Oh, Allah!' a woman breathed. 'There will be fighting, the soldiers will sack and loot the city .... We are all going to die!'

'We should all stay inside and keep our doors locked,' another woman joined in. 'The city will be very unsafe with angry soldiers wandering around.'

Just then, a man who had a shop near the fort came rushing into the courtyard and gave them the details of the sepoys' hold over the Red Fort. They had occupied the gardens and pavilions, and had killed all the English people who were inside the fort, including some women. A few sepoys had also started riding around the Jama Masjid, looking for the English and Christians. Hearing this, the crowds fell silent, the air turning heavy with dread.

Then Sadiq's mother turned to Bishnu's in panic. 'My husband! He's out there on the streets—he'll get killed!'

'Of course not!' Bishnu's father said quietly. 'Why should anyone kill a poor tonga-wallah? I'll go and look for him right now.' He turned to Bishnu. 'Put the vegetables inside.' And he hurried away.

Soon after, the boys slipped out of the house and ran to the corner where the tongas usually waited for passengers.

Sadiq asked a tonga-wallah, 'Chacha, have you seen my abbu anywhere?'

'He took a fare to Ballimaran, beta . . .'

Before the man had finished speaking, the boys had run out to the main avenue of Chandni Chowk. Ballimaran was far away—at the other end of the road, near the Fatehpuri Masjid.

They ran and ran and ran, past the shops that were starting to close as the news of the trouble spread. There was panic in the air as people hurried in all directions. The boys jogged past the Sis Ganj Gurdwara, where the Granthis—unaware of what was happening outside—were still singing *shabad*s. Then beyond the kotwali, where they caught a glimpse of policemen running about and shouting at each other, and past the Sunehri Masjid, where people were huddling by the steps. Finally, the boys stopped to rest, leaning against a tree, panting and covered in sweat. Ballimaran was still so far away.

Suddenly Sadiq shouted, 'ABBU!', pointing at a tonga coming towards them. The boys sprinted across and ran up to the middle of the road, jumping and waving to make the tonga stop.

'What's the matter? Have you gone mad?' Sadiq's father pulled the reins hard to stop the horse. 'You could get hurt. What are you two doing here, so far away from home?'

'War!' panted Sadiq. 'The gora paltan is here!'

'The sipahis are killing the angrez in the Laal Qila!' Bishnu jumped up and down in a panic.

'What did you say?' a voice spoke from the back of the tonga, and a handsome white-bearded man leaned forward. 'What gora paltan?'

'Wait! Wait! Let me move the tonga . . .' Sadiq's father took the tonga to the side of the road and parked it as the boys scrambled on board, talking away and nearly breathless with anxiety.

After listening to their report, 'But why?' the old man asked, puzzled. 'Why are the sipahis doing this? They are usually such loyal soldiers.'

'I'd heard some time back that there was some problem with the new rifles that they had been given,' Sadiq's father muttered.

'But kill the English!' the old man exclaimed. 'They will be slaughtered if they do that. The Company Bahadur is very powerful.'

Sadiq's father turned to the old man. 'Huzoor, I think you should go back home. The city is not safe today.'

'You are right. Let's go back. Oh, I am so worried about the badshah!' the white-bearded man said anxiously. 'He is very old and not well. I was planning to visit him today. I hope the sipahis treat him with respect . . .'

The tonga now turned around, towards Ballimaran. Bishnu, who by now was sitting at the back of the tonga, next to the old man, opened his eyes wide. 'You know the badshah, huzoor?'

'Yes, I do. We meet often to talk about poetry. You know he writes poetry under the name Zafar?'

Bishnu shook his head.

'You are a poet like him?' asked Sadiq, who was sitting in front and had turned to stare at the old man.

'Yes. Do you two like reading poems?' the old man asked.

'Nah! I can't read or write, huzoor.' Sadiq grinned and then nodded towards Bishnu. 'Neither can he.'

By then, the tonga was entering the lane called Ballimaran.

'Then why don't you two come to my house and I'll teach you to read and write? I live right here in Ballimaran.'

The boys exchanged a quick glance. Sit at home and read books? When there were marbles and gilli-danda to be played and kites to be flown? Hardly!

'Whom will we ask for, huzoor, in Ballimaran?' Bishnu asked politely.

'Oh, everyone knows my house. Just ask for Ghalib's haveli and they will point it out to you.' Just then, the tonga came to a stop at the doorway of a haveli. Ghalib stepped down and, after paying his fare, turned to the boys. 'So you two will come to study?'

'We'll think about it, huzoor,' Sadiq said respectfully, not sounding keen at all.

'Maybe we will . . . but I am not too sure.' Bishnu nodded in agreement.

Mirza Mohammad Asadullah Khan Ghalib, the greatest poet of Delhi, laughed and walked away.

Historical Note

Mirza Mohammad Asadullah Khan Ghalib (1797–1869) was the greatest poet in the court of the last Mughal emperor, Bahadur Shah Zafar. The king was also a poet and was Ghalib's patron. Ghalib's lyrical poems, called ghazals, are sung even today, and the shers, or couplets, are considered classics of Urdu literature. Ghalib is buried near the dargah of the Sufi saint Sheikh Nizamuddin Auliya in Delhi.

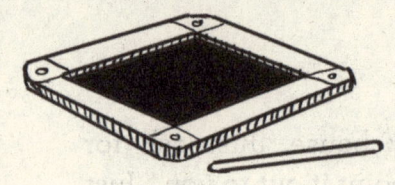

A DISOBEDIENT GIRL

Ma says I am a vain little girl because I like writing my name. One day she was flipping through my handwriting notebook and saw that I had written my name on top of every page—Bindubashini Debi... Bindubashini Debi... Though she did admit that my Bengali handwriting was really improving. I like names, so I wrote hers and Baba's too—Sri Ramnarayan and Srimati Indubala Mukhopadhyay.

Baba says Bindubashini is much too long a name for a nine-year-old girl who is four feet tall. So he calls me Bindi. I had to correct him. I am nine-*and-a-half* years old and four feet and *eight* inches tall. Of course, I allowed him to call me Bindi.

One morning as Baba sat in his easy chair, sipping tea and reading the newspaper, I was sitting on the windowsill, scribbling on my slate.

The chalk was squeaking and screeching as I did the division sums he had given me. Suddenly he said, 'Bindi, how would you like to write your name in English?'

'Oh, I would like it very much, Baba!'

Ma, who was standing by the bed, folding clothes, stopped. 'English?'

'Maybe it's time our Bindi went to school.'

'School?' Ma stared at him. 'Why can't you teach her? You know no girl from this family has ever been to school.'

'Well, then it's time they did.' Baba flapped his newspaper and folded it on another page. 'For how long are we going to stay in the last century? This is 1872 and we have good schools for girls in Calcutta now.'

'And you think your mother will let Bindi go to school? You remember what happened when you taught me English?'

'Oh yes, I do! So we'll have a repeat of that. What's the problem?'

I hopped down and went and leaned against Baba. I was feeling a bit puzzled. 'If Ma could learn English, why can't I?'

'Exactly! So next week, Miss Bindubashini Debi, you are going to learn English at Hindu Balika Vidyalaya.'

Ma sighed. She always sighs like that when Baba is being stubborn. Then I forgot all about it because I was feeling so very excited about going to school.

Sometimes it is quite useful to be four feet and eight inches tall because people don't always notice you. Also, the adults in the family think I'm too young, and that, being a girl, I'm too stupid to understand anything anyway. But I *do* understand a lot, and I remember what I hear, and I tell Ma and Baba about it later.

That morning after Baba left for work, Ma was busy in the kitchen. I was playing with my dolls behind a pillar in the veranda, which is right in front of Grandma's puja room. My grandma is always right there, sitting in front of the huge silver stand on which were all these idols of gods and goddesses. Today she was there with my aunt—Shaila Pishi. Pishi is Baba's younger sister. I know all their names too: My aunt is Shaila Bala Debi and my grandma is Mokshada Sundari.

Last year, Pishi's husband died, and she came back to stay with us . . . forever. Grandma calls her a 'widow'. Earlier Pishi used to wear these lovely

Tangail saris in bright colours and lots of jewellery, but the day she came back—when she stepped down from the horse-drawn carriage—I saw that she was wearing a snow-white sari. That night Baba got very angry at Grandma because she wanted Pishi to not only cut off all her hair but also shave her head like Grandma has always done since she became a widow. But Baba stopped her, and so Pishi got to keep her hair but had to give up her lovely saris and jewellery. Now Grandma makes her work all day in the kitchen and then do hours and hours of puja. Before her marriage, Pishi used to sing as she worked around the house. She doesn't any more.

So that morning, as I was playing with my dolls in the veranda, Grandma was stringing a jasmine garland in the puja room. I heard her say, 'Have you heard what they are planning to do with Bindi?'

Pishi was grinding sandalwood. 'No.'

'Your brother wants to send her to school!'

'Oh really?' Pishi's hands stilled as she stared at Grandma. 'Remember, he wanted to send me to school too? But you stopped him. Are you going to do that *again*?'

'Of course I will! A girl from the Mukhopadhyay family going to school? What would people say!'

'I remember what *you* said. That educated girls gain bad karma when they leave their homes to go to school. And then that mysterious karma makes them widows because it takes the lives of their husbands.'

Grandma glared at Pishi. 'What are you trying to say, Shaila?'

'I never went to school but I still became a widow, didn't I?'

'Who can fight one's karma? Our pandit says you must have done something truly evil in your last birth—'

'Your pandit took a bundle of cash to read my horoscope. Then how is it that he didn't spot a dead husband in it? Or find all that evil karma?'

'I don't care what you or your precious brother thinks! It is written in our sacred books that girls who go to school always become widows,' Grandma snapped back.

Pishi laughed. 'But *you* can't read, Ma! How do you know?'

After lunch, Pishi came to our room, pulled my pigtails, tickled me and made me giggle. 'Now, who's going to school?'

'Me!' I leaned against her lap as she and Ma sat on the four-poster bed and began playing cards.

Ma chewed paan and said, 'So you know? Did your brother tell you?'

'No. Your revered mother-in-law did.'

I've noticed that nowadays she always calls Grandma 'the revered mother-in-law' and it makes Ma laugh. I studied Pishi's cards as I have started to understand this game and pointed to a six of spades. Pishi slapped it down and won the hand and said I was a clever girl.

'First Dada tried to send me to school when I was Bindi's age. Then he taught you English and now this. Ma is waiting for society to collapse around us.'

'How did she stop you from going to school?' Ma wanted to know.

'Oh! At that time, our father was alive and playing God. So a lot of weeping and wailing did the trick. Dada was still in college, and after a while he couldn't fight them any more because Father threatened to throw him out of the house. But every evening he sat with me and taught me himself. Ma didn't like that one bit.'

Ma began to look worried. 'So you think she will try again?'

'Oh yes!' exclaimed Pishi. 'But things are different now. Dada is earning well and it is his money that really runs this house. Also, my father is not around.'

Ma had stopped playing. 'But there will be trouble?'

'You can be sure of that! Do you think my dear mother, elder brother and his lovely wife will stay quiet?'

I curved my neck to look up at Pishi's face. 'Trouble over me?'

She kissed my nose. 'You are the troublesome daughter of a very troublesome man, my darling Bindi Begum.'

'No, I am not!'

'Oh no . . .' Ma sighed. 'I suppose it will all start at dinner.'

'Quite possible, and I'm going to have fun!'

I don't always understand what Pishi says. When have I ever been a troublesome girl?

So that night I was in the dining room well before everyone else. In our family, the men and children eat first. The women do all the cooking, serve us and then eat much later . . . well, almost all the women. Grandma makes Pishi keep all these fasts, so on many days, after spending hours in the kitchen, Pishi does not eat at all. Grandma says widows don't feel hungry.

In the dining room, the places had been laid: five small carpets on the floor with brass thalis and bowls next to them. The seats were for my uncle, Baba, my two cousins and me. I went and sat at the end of the row. My uncle is Baba's older brother and he has two sons, and I know all their names—Ramanath,

Radhanath and Sitanath, and my *jethi*, my uncle's wife, is Chunibala Debi. My cousins—I call them Radhu Dada and Situ Dada—now go to college, so they've *both* gone to school. But then they are boys, and the boys in our family are educated.

My aunt and Ma served us: first, the pinch of salt, the slices of lemon, then the puffed-up puris and vegetable fries. Then Pishi served the rice, dal and potato curry. Finally, Ma brought the fish cooked in mustard sauce. All the while Grandma stood in one corner, telling her prayer beads and watching the women to make sure they served us properly. I knew Pishi had cooked the fish curry but she wouldn't be allowed to eat it. She'd only get the vegetables, if she was not fasting, that is.

My uncle dipped a puri in the dal and, turning to Baba, spoke behind his drooping moustache, 'What is this I hear, Ramnarayan?'

Baba bit into a brinjal fry. 'What have you heard?'

'You are sending your daughter to school!'

'Ah! Ma has already complained, has she?' Baba chewed on.

My uncle was still staring at Baba. 'Are you or are you not sending the girl to school?'

'Correct! I am.'

My uncle stopped eating. 'Are you mad?'

'Not that I am aware of.'

'What's the need for her to go to school? Instead, you should be looking for a good boy for her. She'll be ten soon . . . she is getting too old for marriage. My daughters were married by the time they were nine!'

'She will not be married till she is at least twelve. I want her to know more about the world first.'

Grandma looked up. 'What do you mean *know* about the world?'

'Bindi's husband will be an educated man, and they should be able to talk to each other, have things in common. Also, she enjoys reading, and English books will improve her mind.'

'Improve her *mind*?' My jethi, who was standing beside Grandma, spoke up. 'Since when do women need minds? All she'll do is cook and bring up children. Girls who are educated become disobedient and refuse to do housework.' She glared at Ma and Pishi. 'Wasting their time reading books and playing cards!'

Baba grinned at my aunt. 'Well, then, Boudi, she'll be a disobedient wife.'

'Like yours?'

'Exactly!'

Suddenly my uncle shouted, making me jump. 'Ramnarayan, I order you to stop! This is against the traditions of the family! It is against our dharma!'

'And what will people say?' Grandma added, just as loudly.

'You can't stop me this time, Ma.' Baba went on eating. 'She's *my* daughter.'

I looked up to where Ma and Pishi stood by the door. Ma had her head down, so I couldn't see the expression on her face. Pishi was standing there, her arms crossed, leaning against the wall, and she had a strange little smile on her face. Maybe she really did find all the trouble a lot of fun.

Baba licked his fingers. 'Who made the fish? Must be you, Shaila. It's delicious!'

But my uncle wouldn't stop. 'Don't forget, our family's reputation will be ruined if you go ahead with this foolishness.'

Then Pishi spoke. 'When you gamble away the family money, Borda, the family's reputation stays intact, but a nine-year-old girl going to school will ruin it?'

'Shaila!' Grandma shouted. 'Leave the room!'

'Well, before you go . . .' Baba grinned up at Pishi. 'Will you give me another piece of fish?'

'With pleasure!' Pishi laughed.

I noticed that Radhu Dada and Situ Dada, who hadn't said a word, looked at each other and exchanged a quick smile.

It looked like I was going to school after all.

In the week before I started school, all I heard in the house were angry comments about what Baba was doing. And every night I reported everything back to him, and he laughed and called me his 'Mukhopadhyay Gazette'. So I asked him what a gazette was and he told me I was a newspaper. How can a girl be a newspaper? He talks such nonsense sometimes.

One morning I was playing with balls of dough in the kitchen, Pishi was cutting vegetables and Malati, our maid, was grinding spices on the huge grinding stone. Grandma says that I will soon have to start learning to cook, so on many mornings I play in the kitchen. I had just told Malati that I was going to Hindu Balika Vidyalaya from Monday, and she stopped working, opened her mouth in a huge 'O', widened her eyes and asked Pishi, 'O, Ma! Is that really true?'

Pishi went on slicing the cabbage. 'Yes.'

'But, Didi, you must stop your brother! This will ruin her life! Who will marry their son to a girl who has gone to school? Do you know, the younger girl of the Roy Choudhuris went to school, and it's only now that they have found a boy for her—and she is fourteen! And the boy lives in Benares! No good Calcutta family was interested.'

Pishi stopped her work and stared straight at Malati. 'Fine! Then we'll find a good Benares boy for Bindi.' Then she smiled in that funny, teasing way she does. 'What a good idea, Malati! Then I can go too and bathe in the Ganga and visit all the temples, and then I'll certainly go straight to heaven.'

Malati glared at Pishi. 'Don't laugh, Didi. This is serious!'

'I'm not laughing. I'm being very serious, just like you.'

On Thursday, when Panditmoshai, our family priest, came to do the Lakshmi Puja, Grandma and my jethi sat whispering with him in the puja room. They did not spot me sitting behind the pillar.

Jethi was very angry. 'A girl of this family going out in public like this . . . it is really shocking! My daughters and I leave the house only in covered palanquins.'

I know that's true because when my jethi wants to take a dip in River Ganga, the palanquin bearers dunk the palanquin in the water with her still inside! Pishi says my jethi will one day go to heaven in a palanquin.

'What will people say?' Grandma cried. *Why does she keep saying that again and again?* 'I'm sure Shaila and Indu have encouraged Ramnarayan to do this!'

'Hardly!' my aunt sniffed. 'Your younger son always starts the trouble and it is he who encourages Shaila and Indu to follow.'

'I keep praying they will have a son,' said Grandma. 'Then they would stop spoiling the girl like this.' That is another thing she says often about Ma and Baba. I don't agree—I'm not spoilt at all.

Panditmoshai, who is fat, with a big belly, did the puja, took the money from Grandma, ate a plateful of fruits and sweets and burped loudly. Then he hurried out to catch Baba as he was leaving for work.

'Ramnarayan, my son! I need to talk to you.'

'I have to go to work, Panditmoshai . . .' Baba kept walking.

Panditmoshai stood before Baba and made him stop. 'It will only take a minute. Your mother is very upset—'

'I know. Tell me, as a Brahmin scholar, what do you think will happen when Bindi goes to school?'

'It is against our dharma, you know that! As our scriptures say, *"Stree buddhi pralayankari"*— a woman's mind is a dangerous and destructive thing. Society will be ruined and dharma will collapse if women are educated.'

'Oh! It will collapse, is it?' Baba stood still and bent his head politely towards Panditmoshai. 'Tell me, which scripture says that?'

'Heh . . . heh . . .' Panditmoshai gave this really oily smile. 'You are always joking . . .'

'No, I am not. I really want to know which Veda, Upanishad or shastra says girls should be kept locked inside their homes like cows in a shed.'

'Oh, leave all the scriptures and pujas to me!' Panditmoshai waved his hand. 'You don't want to bring the curses of all your ancestors on your head.'

'Quite! The same ancestors who would have blessed me fifty years ago if Shaila had been burnt on the funeral pyre of her husband and become sati? Maybe I don't want ancestors like that. Tell me, is there a puja that we can do to get rid of them?'

By now Grandma had come out. 'What are you doing?' she shouted at Baba. 'Apologize immediately to Panditmoshai!'

'Of course. My apologies, sir! But I still want to find the scriptures that say that burning girls is better than educating them. Even an eminent scholar like Raja Ram Mohan Roy searched through all of them but couldn't find any.'

Panditmoshai stood silently before Baba.

'Next Thursday, Panditmoshai, you and I will discuss the shastras.' Then he picked up the edge of his dhoti and strolled off.

I noticed Panditmoshai was sweating as he spoke to Grandma. 'Ma, I will not come to this house again if your son behaves like this . . .' And he hurried away.

'O Panditmoshai!' I called out after him. 'You forgot your umbrella!'

The day I was to go to school, Radhu Dada and Situ Dada sneaked into our room early in the morning and hugged me.

'Don't talk too much in class, Bindi,' Radhu Dada said.

'And obey your teacher,' Situ Dada added.

'Of course I'll obey, what do you think I am? Stupid?'

'One day Bindi will beat you both in maths,' Baba said.

'I know she will.' Situ Dada smiled down at me.

So that morning I didn't really mind that Grandma, my uncle and aunt did not come out to see me off on my first day of school.

The first week in school went by in a whirl. We were taught by Mrs Roy, and we did maths, history, geography, Bengali and began learning the English alphabet. The best thing about school was that I made so many friends! There was Subhashini and Mrinal, Parboti and Madhabilata. Every afternoon, Ma and Pishi would ask what I did in school that day. Then in the evening Baba, Situ Dada and Radhu Dada would ask the *same* questions, and I had to tell them everything *all* over again. Grandma, Uncle and Aunt were not speaking to Ma, Baba, Pishi and me. Baba said it made life very peaceful.

A month later, at dinner, Situ Dada was teaching me the English names of vegetables.

'Aloo is potato, *begoon* is brinjal . . .'

'What's the English for payesh?'

'The English don't eat payesh.'

'Really? No payesh? Oh, that's so sad!'

'Oh, stop it!' my uncle shouted suddenly. 'Let me eat in peace!'

'Why, Jethu?' I asked him. 'Don't you like the English?'

'Quiet, Bindi!' Ma said. 'Eat your food.'

'But, Ma, what about dharma?'

They all stopped eating and turned to stare at me. Then Baba spoke, and his voice shook as he did. I knew he was trying not to laugh. 'What about it?' he asked.

'I've been going to school for a month, Baba, and I'm worried! Remember what Panditmoshai said? That dharma will collapse. Has it collapsed yet?'

Radhu Dada nearly choked on his food. 'Dharma is still alive and kicking, Bindi.'

But why was Pishi holding her sari over her mouth and giggling? I wasn't joking!

'But I'm worried about Mrs Roy . . . I've told you about her so many times. Didu says women become widows when they go to school, and Mrs Roy has even gone to college! So when dharma collapses, will her husband die?'

Radhu Dada coughed, then drank some water. Why were his shoulders shaking like that? Was he laughing at me again?

'I told you!' Grandma scowled. 'The moment you send a girl to school, they become disobedient and start asking questions. One month in school, and she has already become troublesome!'

'And isn't that wonderful, Dada?' Pishi smiled at Baba, who smiled back. 'Finally we have a disobedient girl.'

Ma said, 'Bindi, no more talking. Eat your payesh.' So I did, very obediently.

Historical Note

This story is set in the last decades of the nineteenth century, when girls began to go to school in Bengal. At that time, there was strict purdah and women were not allowed to leave their houses. They spent their lives working in the kitchen and caring for the family. The condition of widows in Bengal was shameful, as they were treated like slaves.

There was a huge opposition to women's education by orthodox people, who said that educated girls were unlucky, that often their husbands died young and that it was against Hindu dharma. Also, the older women declared that educated girls became disobedient and refused to do housework.

The movement for the rights of women was led by men who'd received Western education, who realized that if Indian society was to progress, women needed to be emancipated. Raja Ram Mohan Roy fought against the terrible practice of sati, in which widows were burnt alive on the funeral pyres of their husbands. Ishwar Chandra Vidyasagar fought for widows to be remarried, and he and the members of the Brahmo Samaj, a society started by Ram Mohan Roy to reform Hinduism, opened many schools for girls.

This was the beginning of women's emancipation in Bengal, but one must remember that no one was yet talking of women's equality. Though women were offered a basic education, they were still expected to be obedient to men and just stay wives and mothers. Still, it was a start, because when girls became educated, they began to question how society treated them. The fight for equality would be fought a century later, and it would be led by women.

And the struggle still goes on.

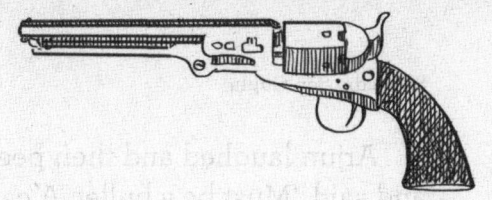

THEY FOUGHT LIKE TIGERS

Ancient brick walls loomed around them and the empty arches of doors and windows led into dim, echoing rooms, many without a roof. They were wandering in the garden, where squirrels ran up and down the shady peepul and jamun trees and pigeons fluttered about and perched on broken carvings as the winter sun filled the air with a mellow golden warmth. For a place that had known war and death, it was a surprisingly serene and welcoming one.

It was an interesting spot for a school outing.

Ira touched a patch of shattered bricks in a wall and wondered aloud, 'Do you think a cannonball did this or a bullet?'

'Who knows?' Shahid shrugged and said with dancing eyebrows, 'To me it's just a 150-year-old hole in the wall!'

Arjun laughed and then peered closer at the hole and said, 'Must be a bullet. A cannonball would make a much larger hole, won't it?'

They had wandered away from the green lawns of the old Residency in Lucknow and now moved deeper into the ruined buildings. Something dark and fluttering flew past Arjun's face and he ducked nervously. *'What was that?* A bat?'

As they walked through the silent destroyed rooms, the sun slipped behind a passing cloud and the air turned dank, dark and gloomy. In the fading light, Ira peered at a small booklet and read aloud, 'The Siege of the English Residency began after the sepoys of Lucknow revolted on the night of 30 May 1857. For nearly five months the sepoys surrounded the Residency, and during this time all the English soldiers, officials and their families lived under siege. There was fierce fighting before the East India Company's army arrived and rescued the people who were trapped inside. At one time, there were nearly 3000 people inside, including officers, soldiers, servants, women and children—'

'The children began to die first...' said a quavering voice from somewhere in the gloom behind them, making the three jump in fright.

They turned nervously to see a white-haired old man sitting on what looked like a truly antique and very tatty old sofa in the corner. Very, very carefully

they went closer to get a better look, because the man was very hard to see in the dark. Shahid thought that the wavy grey shadows around him were somehow moving gently and the old man seemed to swim in and out of view.

Ira frowned, trying to get a clearer image, but the man seemed to be like a reflection in moving water, appearing and disappearing. She couldn't even make out if he was young or old, because sometimes the face seemed much younger and at others, wrinkled and old. He looked sort of harmless, though, leaning on his walking stick and looking up at them with a slight smile.

'Which children?' Arjun asked politely. 'You mean the children in the Residency when the sepoys laid the siege?'

'Correct! The soldiers were dying from bullet wounds, and the women and children from cholera, typhoid and small pox.' He gave a shrug. 'The food and medicine began to run out. Only a third survived the siege . . . It was terrible!'

Shahid, never too interested in history, decided to change the subject—all the talk of death and dying was getting sort of depressing. 'Well, sir . . .' he began, 'tell me something. After the siege was over, why didn't the people of Lucknow repair this house? Look at the walls and pillars! We need to cement them real fast or they'll collapse any day!'

The old man gave a short laugh. 'The English wouldn't let them. We wanted to keep it exactly the way it was when Sir Colin Campbell arrived with his troops and lifted the siege, letting us evacuate everyone. We defeated the rebels, and this,' he waved an arm around him, 'is a monument to our victory. We won!'

They stared at him, very puzzled, as the image of the man seemed to sharpen a little. Ira looked closely at the ancient face before her. He had spotty pale skin, a white moustache drooping over narrow lips and a straggly beard. He had a bald head and lines around the eyes; a veined hand was shaking a little, clasped tightly over the walking stick.

'*We? We defeated the rebels?*' she asked, a bit irritated. 'Who's "we"?'

'Us. The English.'

'Ah! So you're an Englishman and you think the Indian sepoys were rebels who deserved to be killed!' Ira asked hotly.

'But you forget, this is our country,' Arjun joined in.

'And you English folks came and colonized us,' Shahid added grimly. 'The sepoys were *not* rebels, they were fighting for their nawab, Wajid Ali Shah of Lucknow.'

'*And* the Mughal badshah Bahadur Shah Zafar.'

'Quite! You are absolutely correct.' The old man raised a hand to calm them. 'They were not rebels, and oh yes! They were very, *very* brave and nearly defeated us. They fought like tigers even though they did not have enough ammunition or good officers.' Then he leaned forward and said, 'But do you know that everyone did not want the Indian rulers back? That there were Indian soldiers inside the Residency fighting to protect the English.'

The three of them stared at him in surprise and then Ira said softly, 'They didn't teach us that in school. I thought there were only English troops here.'

'Of course not! In Lucknow, Delhi, Kanpur, Gwalior—you name it—sepoys loyal to the East India Company fought against the rebel sepoys. Sikhs, Pathans and Gurkha soldiers against Awadhis and Biharis.' He began to laugh at their shocked faces, showing large yellowing teeth.

By now even Shahid had become interested, and they were all sitting cross-legged on the floor, at the old man's feet. Shahid leaned forward and asked, 'Why? Why did they stay loyal?'

'Well, everyone did not want the old kings back.'

'You mean Wajid Ali Shah?'

'Don't get me wrong, old Wajid Ali was a charming man . . .' There was a nostalgic gleam in the old man's eyes. 'Sang beautifully and a lovely poet too, but he was so very lazy. He spent all his time with the dancing girls and musicians; he wasn't interested in running the kingdom at all!'

'But there was also Bahadur Shah in Delhi. Wasn't he a good king?'

'The Sikhs did not think so. The Mughals had executed their gurus, and they had been fighting the Mughals for years. They didn't want the Mughals back. But, ah!' The old man smiled, as if he suddenly recalled a very pleasant memory. 'Now, things would have been very different if *she* would have been the nawab of Lucknow!'

They leaned forward eagerly. 'SHE? Who was "she"?'

'Begum Hazrat Mahal, Wajid Ali's wife. What an amazing lady!'

'You think Hazrat Mahal would have made a great ruler?' Ira was very interested.

'Oh, absolutely! She used to run the kingdom anyway, while Wajid Ali was busy with his poetry mushairas. She was courageous, smart and hard-working. In fact, the two bravest rebels were Begum Hazrat Mahal and that young queen of Jhansi ... now, what was her name?' He knitted his snowy brows. 'A pretty thing!'

'Rani Laxmi Bai!' the three prompted together.

'Correct! These two women were brave as lions. If they could have ruled their kingdoms while we had our queen Her Majesty Queen Victoria in England ...' he gave a short barking laugh, 'the world would have been a much better place. You can be sure of that!'

'I think I like you, sir!' Ira grinned up at him.

'Women! Hmm ... sensible creatures. They almost never go to war, and they care for the people much more than the men.'

'You are *sooo* right!' Ira nodded and stuck out her hand. 'Let me shake your hand, sir! You're a wonderful man!'

The old man laughed again and, reaching out, shook her hand. Ira felt it like the soft, fleeting touch of a feather brushing across her palm, and then her arm tingled a bit. She looked up in surprise at the old man ... Did he wink at her?

'So, sir,' Shahid said firmly, 'you obviously support the East India Company and not the Indian kings.'

'Wrong! I support none of them because the badshahs, rajas, nawabs or the East India Company—no one really cared for the people of this wonderful country. The people deserved better than the kings they got, and the Company officers were only interested in making money. None of them tried to help the people. The peasants stayed as poor as before, they starved and died in famines and no one came to help. Why do you think poor villagers joined the Company army and became sepoys? Just to survive. And then the Company officers treated them like slaves.'

'So you believe in democracy, huh?' Arjun grinned.

'And in Gandhiji?' Ira grinned too.

By then the old man had stood up and was limping slowly towards the open door. 'Democracy in India? People getting the vote?' they heard him mumble. 'Not a bad idea actually, but who's this Gandhi fellow?'

As he reached the door, his dark, stooped figure stood out against the pale, grey winter light outside. And again they thought they saw the shadows swaying all around him, breaking the edges of his figure, turning him into an odd shimmering, changing shape.

'Sir!' Shahid called out loudly from behind. 'Hey, Mr Englishman! Who are you? You never told us your name!'

The old man did not turn but raised an arm to wave goodbye and then said something softly under his breath. It sounded like '... Law ... rence ...'

Just then, the sun came out and the light turned so bright that the doorway glowed in the golden glitter. It dazzled their eyes and made them blink. When they looked again, the old man was gone.

They glanced around the room. The sofa on which the old man had been sitting had vanished! They ran out to the garden and looked around, but the old man was nowhere in sight.

'What did he say his name was?'

'Something Lawrence, I think.'

'Lawrence?' Ira turned to stare at Arjun and Shahid. 'Are you sure? What Lawrence?'

'Harry . . . Henry . . . something like that.' Shahid shrugged. 'Why are you getting so excited, yaar?'

'*Henry Lawrence?* Did he say Henry Lawrence?' Ira's eyes were wide with astonishment. 'Oh! That can't be!'

'Why not?' Arjun frowned.

'Don't you remember? We saw the grave of Henry Lawrence, the last resident of Lucknow, in the cemetery just now and I read out the gravestone?'

They ran back to the ancient graveyard of the ruined church behind the Residency and stared at the stained stone gravestone. It said:

Here lies
Henry Lawrence
Who tried to do his duty.

'Oh my God!' Arjun's eyes were wide with shock. '*That* Henry Lawrence died right here in 1857 at the Siege of the Lucknow Residency!'

'Nah!' Shahid shook his head. 'I can't believe that! No way!'

'He did keep sort of vanishing into the shadows, didn't he?' Arjun said softly. 'I often couldn't see him properly.'

Ira shivered. 'And he did look really, really old.'

'Well, yes. And also, at times . . .' Shahid said with a shiver, 'he looked sort of younger . . .'

The three stood staring all around the empty sunlit garden. Was that an echoing, barking laugh fading away in the distance?

Historical Note

Just before the Uprising of 1857, the East India Company banished Wajid Ali Shah, the nawab of Lucknow, to Calcutta. During the uprising, the rebellious sepoys laid siege to the English Residency in Lucknow, and Queen Hazrat Mahal supported them. But when the uprising failed, she escaped to Nepal and later died there. Wajid Ali died in Calcutta, and Lucknow never had a nawab again.

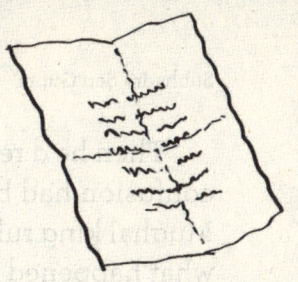

ROHAN AND MR MAJ

The moment Rohan read the three questions on the blackboard, he knew he was in trouble. Not the ordinary, everyday kind of trouble, but the dreadfully serious, not-to-be-laughed-at, getting-detention-after-class kind of trouble. This was a class test, and he had to only answer one question out of three. That should have made it easy, but it did not—because this was a history test.

The first question was 'Why did the Company sepoys decide to ride from Meerut to Delhi in 1857?'

Sepoys... um... Weren't they the guys who started the whole mutiny against the East India Company... The uprising thing? Soldiers, no? This much he did remember, but he had no idea why they'd come to Delhi. And from Meerut? Why? *What were they doing in boring Meerut?*

Then he'd read the second question and the fog of confusion had become deeper. 'Give the name of the Mughal king ruling in 1857. How was he involved and what happened to him after the uprising?'

Ohhh . . . the name's just here . . . He'd reached towards that out-of-reach part of his befuddled brain . . . *Something Khan? Nah! Shah? Yeah, something Shah . . . Can't be Shah Jahan, can it?*

By then Miss Menon had finished writing out the third question. 'Why did the sepoys refuse to use the Enfield rifle?'

Wasn't it something to do with bullets that were covered in animal fat and something about them having to bite them? Slowly a sort of vague answer was appearing on the crumpled-up page of his mind, and finally Rohan decided to answer the last question. He sighed hopelessly, picked up his pen and began to scribble, hunched painfully over his exercise book, as if he had a sudden stomach ache. He always felt like this during a history test.

'I'm going to flunk history big time,' Rohan informed his friend Manpreet later in the afternoon as they kicked around a football in the playing field.

'So what's new about that? You always flunk history.' Manpreet took an experimental kick at the goal and it went wide. 'Miss Menon gets this sad look on her face when she talks to you, as if she's about to cry.'

'That's happened only *once* . . .' Rohan corrected his friend.

'Yeah, right . . . When we had to write about Akbar and the Second Battle of Panipat, you got the date wrong and wrote about Babur and the first battle . . . heh-heh . . .'

'History really sucks!' Rohan dribbled the ball gloomily. 'I can't wait to get to the eleventh, when I can drop the stupid subject. I like science, maths and geography—they are useful subjects. Who needs history anyway?'

Eleventh was months away, and right now there was the problem of Miss Menon. In the next history period, she went around returning the exercise books and when she came to Rohan, she did not look sad at all. In fact, she looked hopping mad. She gave him that scary bug-eyed glare from behind her glasses and then, with gloom and doom dripping from every word, she said, 'Rohan Trivedi, will you meet me after class, please?'

Please? Since when did teachers say please? That did *not* sound good. Rohan knew what would follow when he met Miss Menon—detention assignment; note for parents; no football practice; life was over. Ah, well.

After school, Rohan shuffled into the library, dragging his school bag. In his hand he held his history classwork exercise book, which bore the 8½ out of 20 that he had got in the test as well as the names of two books he had to consult in the library to write an essay of 500 words on the Uprising of 1857. He also had to include quotations to prove that he had at least opened the two books.

The fat mud-coloured *Advanced History of India* by Majumdar, Datta and Raychaudhuri was easy to find. The second book he was looking for was called *1857* by Surendranath Sen. Rohan noticed that all the writers were Bengali and wondered, *Don't Bongs have anything better to do than write these five-kilo books?*

Rohan did not like libraries—gloomy, grungy places smelling of old paper and cobwebs—and their library could win a prize for dust collection. The tall wooden stacks stuffed with books loomed around him like a jungle in the afternoon light as Rohan bent low and peered at the lower shelves, where the light of the buzzing tube light barely reached.

'Oye, Mr Sen . . . Where *are* you?' He hummed under his breath to stop himself from absolutely dying of boredom. It was a sunny winter afternoon outside, perfect for football, and here he was, looking for some strange book about long-dead people. So Rohan silently asked some questions about history that he never had the courage to ask Miss Menon in class.

What is the point of studying history anyway?

Who thought kids would like to learn about Ashoka's religious policy?

Will the world come to an end if you think that the Second Battle of Panipat was fought in 1756?

Rohan finally found the book at the back of the lowest shelf, where it had fallen behind the stack and got wedged against the wall. It was very hard to spot. Luckily he saw the title '1857', which was printed in big bold letters, and when he managed to pull it out, a puff of dust told him that no one had borrowed it in years. He slapped the book against his leg and looked at it. The volume wasn't as thick as *An Advanced History of India*, but it had the same deadly dull look. It had a grey cover with the title in black and no pictures anywhere. If the cover was so utterly boring, he was sure the inside would be worse.

Miss Menon really had it in for him. This felt like revenge.

Five minutes later, he was sitting at one of the rickety wooden tables, and he decided to open Surendranath Sen first. He had no intention of sitting and reading those books, of course. His plan was to quickly copy down some lines as quotations and then check out the chapter on 1857 in his textbook at home and do the 500 words as fast as he could. This system had worked before.

As he opened the book, more dust floated up, making him sneeze, and that was when he spotted the yellowed sheet of paper sticking out between the pages. It was a thick sheet of handmade paper, folded in four, and as he unfolded it, the paper crackled under his fingers. Rohan opened it optimistically, hoping for something interesting, like maybe a love letter to Miss Menon from the drama coach, Mr Costello. He was sure there was something going on between them.

Well, it wasn't. There were six lines written by hand in this really clear, old-fashioned script in jet-black ink and, squinting slightly, he began to read them, the weird, dated words making him mutter a puzzled 'What the hell . . .' He slowly read aloud:

Take a step beyond mere time,
Be a voyager into endless space.
Say I am free to soar and fly,
I am not tied to any place.
Leaving my mortal being behind,
I move with courage and with grace.

Then there were two lines in Sanskrit:

Om Prithvi! Om Srishti! Om Vyom!
Om Akash! Om Vayu! Namah Shivayah!

Just as Rohan finished reading out the lines, the lights in the library suddenly dimmed and then became very bright, as if there was a sudden power surge. Then the sound of the tube light above him got louder, hissing and buzzing like a malevolent swarm of bees.

Confused, Rohan looked up at the buzzing tube light, when suddenly a high-pitched voice spoke in an excited shout behind him, making him jump. 'You found it, boy! YOU FOUND IT!'

Rohan sprang up and whirled around to find an old man standing behind him—his thin face split by this totally crazy grin—and dancing on his toes in this mad way, as if he were walking on hot coals. The light made his bald head gleam and it shone off his big, thick-framed glasses, making them glitter.

'Where was it?' the dancing man was now chanting. 'Boy, where was it? Was it inside that book?'

Slightly stunned by the wildly waving arms and the whirling eyeballs, Rohan mumbled nervously, 'Er . . . what?'

'Where . . . *where* did you find it, boy?' the old man repeated, nearly frothing at the mouth.

'Come again?' Rohan requested. 'Found what?'

'That paper!' The old man pointed to the sheet with the poem still clutched in Rohan's hand. 'Tell me, boy!'

'My name is Rohan, not Boy,' he corrected the lunatic with a severe frown, 'and who are you?'

'Who are you, *sir*,' the old man corrected him. His eyes had sharpened in this impatient, irritated way behind his glasses.

'What?' He really had to stop saying 'what' in this idiotic manner, Rohan thought absently.

'You call me sir.'

'Why?' Now that was an improvement.

'Because I am your teacher, that's why.'

'No, you're not!' he protested hotly. 'I've never seen you before, and I've been in this school since nursery, *sir*,' he ended sarcastically.

'I was a teacher here a long time ago.'

They stood and stared at each other. Rohan finally took a close look at the old man. He was quite tall and very thin, and he stooped a little; the bony shoulders curved forward, and his head was bald as an egg; his grey trousers were baggy at the knees, as if he hadn't ironed them in months; his dark-blue cotton shirt had a pocket with two pens stuck in it and the pockets of his ancient black cardigan sagged with things stuffed inside; the narrow, high-cheekboned face had firm lips and the large, deep-set eyes behind the glasses were bright with intelligence. He sort of looked like a teacher, Rohan decided—he had that awful *teacherly* look. Maybe it would be safer to stop being too clever with him.

'I'm Rohan Trivedi, sir. Class 10 C.'

'Girish Kumar Majumdar. I used to teach history.' The old man gave a sudden guffaw. 'Long before you were born.'

'Here? In my school?'

'Correct! In the senior Higher Secondary classes.' Then he held out an eager hand. 'That paper, it belongs to me. Can I have it, please? I've been looking for it for years and years.'

Rohan looked down at the sheet of paper and thought, *This could easily belong to this old bozo. Maybe I should give it to him before he has a heart attack or something.*

Just then, he got a flashback of the lecture that he had just got from Miss Menon—all about 'discipline' and 'diligence'. Then there was all that headachy stuff about being 'careless' and 'not serious', and his 'lack of effort'. And this chap was saying that he was a retired history teacher when Rohan was in *no mood* to be obedient to history teachers. So, instead of handing the sheet over, he folded it and slipped it inside the pocket of his school blazer.

Rohan gave Mr Majumdar a cool, weighing look from under his eyelids. 'How do I know it belongs to you . . . sir?'

'I wrote it.' And Mr Majumdar recited the first two lines that Rohan had just read. 'I forget the rest. One day while working here, I must have put it inside this book, and I haven't been able to find it since.'

Rohan could understand that. 'The book had fallen behind the shelf. I had to push the bookcase to reach it.'

'Why were you looking for it?' Mr Majumdar's eyes had sharpened in this very teacher-like way. 'Surendranath Sen in Class 10? That's hard to believe.'

'History project,' Rohan said quickly.

'*Really?*' Clearly Mr Majumdar did not believe him and, before Rohan could stop him, the old man had picked up Rohan's exercise book and begun flipping through the pages. 'Eight and a half on twenty?' He looked up and grinned. 'Detention, isn't it, you nincompoop?'

Now, that sounded like an insult, even though Rohan wasn't sure what the word 'nincompoop' meant. He had to remember to check in the dictionary. 'Yeah, detention. Five hundred words on 1857.' *This Mr Maj is a sharp one*, Rohan thought. *He doesn't miss a trick.* Then, suddenly, he got one of his rare brainwaves.

'Mr Maj, er . . . sir . . . you taught history, right?' The old man nodded. 'So you know everything about the 1857 Uprising . . . Delhi and Meerut and all that stuff?' The eyes narrowed as Mr Maj nodded again. 'Well, then, here's the deal. If you write the 500 words for me, I'll give you the poem.'

'If I wrote it, you moronic bit of ectoplasm,' now Mr Maj was back to glaring and Rohan, who was good at science and knew very well what ectoplasm meant, flinched, 'your teacher will know immediately that you did not do it. Because you write pure garbage.'

Then Mr Maj read aloud what Rohan had written earlier that day. 'The Enfield rifle was a famous rifle made by the Enfield Company of England. They also made bullets covered in fat that the Indian sepoys did not like. So the sepoys got very angry in 1857 and also they wanted to go to Delhi . . . *Pure, unadulterated*

213

garbage, Mr Trivedi! Some of the worst I've read in my long career.'

'Okay, but at least you can help me write the essay,' Rohan said cleverly and then pulled out the poem, waving it temptingly before Mr Maj's eyes. 'You want this, don't ya, Mr Maj?'

That was a mistake because, with surprising speed, the old man reached out and snatched the paper from Rohan's hand and, unfolding it, began to slowly read aloud the poem in this rolling, oratorical style. Rohan stretched out his arm, trying to grab the paper, but Mr Maj swerved away like a boxer ducking from a left hook. Then as he began to back away rapidly from Rohan, the boy lunged forward and clutched at Mr Maj's arm to stop him from running away.

All the while, the old man had been reciting away in this deep, theatrical voice. 'Take a step beyond mere time . . .' Then, exactly when he reached the last line, Rohan began urgently, 'Mr Maj, please don't go away. You have to help me, please, sir! I really know nothing about the . . .'

So just as Mr Maj intoned, 'Om Vayu! Namah Shivayah!' Rohan said '. . . sepoys . . . or Delhi in 1857 . . .'

Suddenly things went totally and absolutely freakishly insane.

Everything began to whirl around as Rohan clutched at Mr Maj's bony arm in complete panic. What was happening? Earthquake? Cyclone? Tsunami?

The bookcases, walls, windows, tables, chairs, even the library assistant at the counter were moving! Why were they all spinning around as if swept up by a tornado? Then it all started to go faster and faster until it was just a swirl of colours, and Rohan closed his eyes in sheer terror.

He could smell smoke, flowers, coffee and fried pakoras. Then he heard the echoing sound of drums, car horns, barking dogs and what seemed to be people singing . . . bhajans! *What is* happening, *bhai?* Rohan thought in alarm.

Then he heard Mr Maj shouting triumphantly, 'It's working! It's working!' and all Rohan could do was keep a desperate hold of Mr Maj's cardigan sleeve, feeling both scared and oddly exhilarated, as if they were on a mad rollercoaster ride.

Suddenly it all stopped, and the echoing silence was somehow just as scary, like being stuck inside a dark tunnel. Rohan took a deep breath and very, very carefully opened his eyes and asked nervously, 'Mr Maj, you there?'

Rohan was still clutching Mr Maj's cardigan sleeve but something felt different now. He glanced at Mr Maj's thin arm and blinked in confusion—he remembered the cardigan being black wool, but now he was holding a sleeve made of soft blue cotton. He looked up and nearly fainted in shock. Mr Maj had changed! *Totally!*

The old man stood before him looking very thrilled. He was now wearing a dark-blue long-sleeved kurta, loose black pyjamas and a white cotton cap. He wore rings on his fingers; golden studs gleamed in his ears; and his shoes had pointy toes. He looked like he was playing a part in a historical serial on television. The only odd thing about him was that, funnily, he still wore his thick black-framed spectacles.

'When did you change your clothes?' Rohan asked, amazed.

'So did you . . . heh-heh . . .' Mr Maj let out a cackle. 'You look very Mughal, my boy!'

Rohan looked down to check what Mr Maj was talking about and froze—he was now wearing a green cotton kurta, white pyjamas and chappals. He touched his head and discovered that his hair was so long that it reached his shoulders, *and* he was wearing earrings!

'What's going on, Mr Maj?' he croaked nervously.

'We've travelled back in time, my boy. Look around you!'

Rohan stood still and stared. They were standing by a wide road with shady trees, at whose end was a huge fortress built of reddish brown stone, a gate and high walls topped with battlements. He knew the fort very well.

'That's the Red Fort . . . Is this Chandni Chowk?'

'Correct! But is it the same as you know it?'

Rohan now surveyed all around him and blinked. 'It's sort of different. All these trees, there are houses next to the fort, that's an open park now . . . oh!' He looked down the road, empty in the early morning hours. 'No cars, no buses, not even cycle rickshaws . . .' Then he saw a man riding by on a bullock cart piled with vegetables, and he too was wearing clothes like his. 'This is not 2018!'

'No, it's not. How clever of you.'

'We are in . . . *the past?* Like when I wasn't even born, eh?'

'Finally, the boy understands! That poem is a magical time-travelling mantra. You say it aloud, name a period and bam! You go back to that time. I was planning to meet Chanakya and Chandragupta Maurya when you yelled, "Delhi! 1857!" And so here we are in the Delhi of 1857.'

'Where are the sepoys? I thought there was a war happening then.'

'Ummm . . .' Mr Maj scratched his ear thoughtfully. 'I think we've got here a bit early. The sepoys will arrive soon enough.' He began walking down Chandni Chowk towards the Red Fort, with Rohan straggling behind.

Rohan was still trying to spot what was different about the place. There was a narrow channel of water running down the middle of the road. On both sides were small, two-storey whitewashed houses, with shops on the ground floor. People were still asleep on charpais laid out on the pavement, and there were *so* many trees—lining the channel and also by the houses. He had a flashback of his last visit to this road, with its heavy traffic and crowds of people surging along the pavements and the air filled with petrol fumes, the sound of rickshaw bells and car horns. Now a man went by riding a horse, and Rohan could smell smoke.

'Smoke?'

'Chullahs. In every kitchen they are lighting the coal and wood chullahs for cooking.'

'That's pollution, no?'

'Delhi has always been smoggy, especially in winters. Even back then they lit fires to keep warm, and, just wait, there will be a traffic jam soon.'

'Here? You're joking!'

'Horses, elephants, palanquins, bullock carts, handcarts, horse-drawn carriages . . . The lanes are narrow and by mid-morning, it'll get pretty crowded.'

'You've been here before?'

'I came to see Shah Jahan and Jahanara once.'

Rohan sniffed. 'I smell puris frying . . .' Flashing his best hungry-puppy smile, he asked, 'How about some breakfast? I'm starving, sir!'

'Good idea. We'd better eat something before things start getting complicated. Those sepoys will really disturb the peace.'

They came to a stop before a street-side food shop. A thin woman in a lehnga–choli was frying puris in a big black iron karahi smoking over an earthen chullah. There stood a row of rickety wooden tables with stools on the pavement, where they sat down. Service was quick as a waiter strolled over and slapped down two brass plates piled with puris, a pumpkin sabji, a dollop of creamy ghee, slices of a mango achar and an earthen bowl of sweet halwa.

'Man! This is yum!' Rohan whistled. He stared at Mr Maj, who was uncharacteristically silent as his mouth was full of food. 'Mr Maj, how come you're still wearing your glasses?'

'That's because they did not have spectacles like these in the nineteenth century. What they did not have does not change. You should be wearing your watch too.'

Rohan pushed back his kurta sleeve and there was his watch, ticking away on his wrist. Only now the date said 11 May and it was 6.30 in the morning. Last he'd checked it had been 5 December and 2 o'clock in the afternoon. He waved for more puris and then asked, 'Tell me, how did you learn this magic-mantra-time-travelling thing?'

'Umm . . . well . . .' Clearly the old man was wondering if he should let Rohan into the secret. He brooded for a while, sucking on a slice of pickled raw mango, and then said, 'Now that you've managed to travel with me, I suppose you have a right to know.' A nostalgic smile curved his lips. 'It all began in 1955. I liked to go hiking in the hills. Do you hike, Rohan?'

'I love to go trekking in the hills, Mr Maj. That's what we call hiking nowadays, and it's great fun.'

The old man frowned at him. 'I've been noticing for some time now that you've been calling me Mr Maj. I don't like it *at all.*'

'Why not? You have a long name—M-A-J-U-M-D-A-A-R! Mr Maj makes you sound like a trendy dude actually.'

'*Trendy? Dude?* What kind of language is that?'

'It's English. The words are in the Oxford Dictionary, if you care to check,' Rohan said shortly. 'In fact, I'm complimenting you.'

Mr Maj scratched his chin. 'Um . . . come to think of it . . . I'm beginning to like Mr Maj . . . sounds sort of pukka sahib.'

'Well, it's better than "sir". Now, you were going to tell me about what happened in 1955,' Rohan prompted gently.

In 1955, Mr Maj, young, fit and with a head of curly black hair, was trekking near Kedarnath in the Himalayas. In those days, there were few roads, and the narrow hill paths seemed to cling to the side of the rocks. On one side were high cliffs and on the other, way, way down below in a deep gorge, was the tumultuous Mandakini River, frothing and swirling away between giant boulders.

'If you took one step wrong, down you'd go,' Mr Maj said. 'It was dangerous, and I loved the challenge.'

The grey granite Kedarnath Temple stood in a valley surrounded by towering snow-capped mountains and among the rocks were caves where ash-smeared sadhus sat meditating. Just for a while, Mr Maj even thought of becoming a sadhu himself because he loved the hills so much.

'Why didn't you?' Rohan tried to imagine a beard below the glasses and long matted locks instead of the bald-as-an-egg head.

'Well ... I had met a girl who later became my wife.' Mr Maj gave a surprisingly sweet smile. 'Mrinalini Mukherji, she taught maths in the middle school.' Rohan nearly choked on a puri but kept a straight face. 'After Kedarnath, I decided to trek further up, on to Gangotri, where the Bhagirathi River appears from a cave above the glacier. You do know that the three rivers Mandakini, Alaknanda and Bhagirathi join to form—'

'River Ganga. I know—geography, I'm good at it. Go on ...'

This was Mr Maj's extraordinary story: When he arrived at Gangotri, the sun was setting and he decided to spend the night in a cave. He found a narrow opening in the rock, crawled in and was unrolling his sleeping bag when a low voice boomed from somewhere deep inside the cave, 'Jai Bholenath!'

Mr Maj peered into the dark and discovered a sadhu sitting before a small fire, smoking a chillum.

Rohan frowned in disapproval. 'Go on.'

The sadhu was thin as a skeleton, with a long white beard and his long hair tied in a topknot. Mr Maj was bundled up in wool in the cold, but the sadhu only wore a cotton dhoti and kurta and had a thin blanket draped across his shoulders.

'I was quite happy to have some company, and he let me take a few drags at his chillum and that warmed me up.'

All this chillum-smoking did not please Rohan. 'Smoking gives you cancer. You know that, right?'

Unfazed by Rohan's disapproval, Mr Maj went on. Clearly, getting cancer did not bother him. 'Then I shared my food with him, and he told me that his name was Sri 108 Bhaveshananda Maharaj . . .'

'That's a stupidly long name. Bhajji for short . . . like the spin bowler,' mumbled Rohan to himself.

'. . . Bhaveshananda grew happier when I pulled out a bottle of brandy, and soon we became friends and he was telling me all about his travels.'

'Where all did Bhajji go?'

'I called him Bhaveshji, you moron, not Bhajji!' snapped Mr Maj. 'And here's how the conversation went all those years ago.' Then Mr Maj repeated their exchange word for word.

Bhaveshji said, 'When I met the Shankaracharya in Badrinath, he was still planning the Vishnu temple there.'

Mr Maj sat up. 'You mean the first . . . *Adi* Shankaracharya?'

Bhaveshji nodded.

'But that was in the eighth century!'

Bhaveshji stroked his thin, straggly beard, a nostalgic smile flickering around his plump lips. 'Ah! I've met them all—the great spiritual teachers of our land—Kabir, Tulsidas, Guru Nanak, Ramakrishna Paramahansa . . .'

'Wait a sec!' Mr Maj's history-teacher brain clicked into action. 'Kabir and Nanak are fifteenth century, Tulsidas is seventeenth century and Ramakrishna is nineteenth century! You've met them all? That is quite impossible, Bhaveshji! I teach history, and I'm not going to get the dates wrong.'

The sadhu gave a benign nod. 'I *have* met them, and so can *you*.'

'I think, Bhaveshji, the smoking and the brandy have got a bit too strong for you. You are having hallucinations, my friend.'

That was when the old sadhu dictated the mantra to him, and Mr Maj wrote it down on a sheet of paper. The next morning, he stood beside the turbulent Bhagirathi River and decided to test it. Within minutes he had zipped back to the third century BCE and seen the battle between Porus and Alexander on the banks of the Jhelum. Then he zipped back to the present. After lunch, he went off to the Raigad Fort in the Western Ghats of Maharashtra and watched Shivaji being crowned king. When he came back, he discovered that Bhaveshji had vanished.

So began Mr Maj's time-travelling hobby. The original mantra was in a very difficult Sanskrit, and as he grew older, he had trouble remembering all the jaw-breaking words correctly. That's why he translated the first six lines into English and discovered, to his delight, that it worked just fine.

'As long as I did the "Om Vayu! Namah Shivayah!" bit in Sanskrit,' Mr Maj ended his fantastic tale, 'I was on my way!'

They had finished their meal of puris by the time the story came to an end, and now Rohan began to feel worried. They had eaten a huge number of puris, but how were they going to pay for it? The waiter cleared the table, slung his duster over one shoulder and said something that sounded like *'Chaar* daam.' *Four what?* Rohan wondered foggily. 'Daam' meant 'price', didn't it?

'Pay him, boy.' Mr Maj waved an airy hand.

'Why? *You* brought me here.'

'Correct! But I have no money.'

'Why not? You're a grown-up. They always have cash.'

'Because I'm a ghost, you oaf! I died a long time ago.'

Rohan stared critically at Mr Maj, who looked pretty solid to him, and then asked in a disbelieving voice, 'You're *dead*, sir? *Really?*'

'Born in 1929—of course I'm dead!'

By then Rohan's heart had begun to thud as the waiter was joined by the thin female cook. The two now stood looming over them, giving them slit-eyed looks, and he noticed that the woman was holding a hot ladle that she was swinging in a threatening way.

'Chaar daam!' the waiter said again.

'I only had sixty-five rupees in school . . .' Rohan could feel beads of sweat dotting his forehead. 'That won't pay for anything!'

Mr Maj grinned. 'Check your pockets.'

To his amazement, Rohan brought out a handful of Mughal coins in copper, silver and one in gold. Mr Maj picked up four small copper coins and gave them to the waiter, who nodded and walked away.

'Food was cheap then.' Mr Maj pointed to the coins. 'Copper daam, silver rupaiya and gold mohur.' He picked up the mohur, a large gold coin with words in the Persian script stamped on one side and a flower on the other, and slipped it into his kurta pocket. 'I'll keep this. There are pickpockets in the bazaar.'

As they walked away from the shop, Rohan remembered something and stopped in his tracks. 'You're a ghost now, Mr Maj?'

'Not in 1857.'

'But in the school library?'

'What year was it then?'

'2018.'

'Oh my sweet Lord, it's the twenty-first century already? I'd really wanted to see the new millennium, but I died in 1996.' As Rohan backed away in alarm, the old man grinned. 'Boy, I'm alive now, just like you. The moment I recite the mantra, I'm flesh and blood again. Why do you think I was looking for that piece of paper?'

They began to walk towards the Red Fort. 'So, where are we going, sir?'

'I think we should go and sit by the Yamuna River and wait for the action to start.'

'What action? *War?*' Rohan wasn't too sure he wanted to be in the middle of a battle of any kind. Violence was not his thing.

'You really know nothing, you dimwit.' Mr Maj clicked his tongue in disapproval. 'Today is 11 May 1857. The day before, on 10 May, the Indian soldiers, called the sepoys, rebelled against their masters of the East India Company at the army barracks in Meerut. They killed the English officers and are now riding towards Delhi at full speed. They'll cross the river by a boat bridge and we'll be there to see them. It will be quite a show, boy!'

Mr Maj and Rohan skirted around the red sandstone walls of the fort and were soon standing on the bank of the Yamuna River. Being summer, it was a narrow, sluggishly flowing stream, and across it was a bridge that made Rohan's eyes brighten with interest.

'Man! That's a cool bridge!'

It was such a clever idea. A row of boats had been tied together all the way across the river and planks of wood had been laid over it to create a floating bridge. People were walking across very easily and, as they watched, a horseman rode slowly across, the bridge swaying and dipping a bit but still staying afloat.

They sat in companionable silence as the sun rose in the sky. Rohan looked around, feeling surprisingly happy. Two men were working nearby in vegetable fields, collecting cabbages and radishes; beyond that, Rohan could see rows of ripening watermelons.

'The watermelons grown on the riverbank are always the sweetest.' Mr Maj sighed.

'Not any more,' Rohan said grimly. 'Now the river is *so* polluted it's covered with a stinky grey froth, and you'd be poisoned by the melons!'

'Froth?' Mr Maj looked puzzled.

'It's the chemicals from the factories that they just let into the river. It's a mess.' Rohan took a deep breath and gave a happy nod. 'The air is so clear here. Do you know Delhi is now the most polluted city in the world? All winter the air is full of this horrid brown smog.'

'Smog that's brown?'

'A filthy, oily thing . . .'

'Really? It's good I'm dead!'

While they had been watching the vegetable farmers, things had started happening at the boat bridge. A group of horsemen had gathered on the opposite bank and now, in small groups, they began to ride carefully across the bridge, which swayed dangerously but held firm. Rohan noticed that many of them were wearing red jackets and white riding breeches. He asked, 'Sepoys?'

'Sepoys!' Mr Maj gave a triumphant laugh, springing to his feet. 'They're here!' They saw that the sepoys were gathering at a small gate, and Mr Maj added, 'That's the riverside gate.' Then he began to hurry towards the gate with Rohan following him.

'What now?' Rohan asked Mr Maj. 'You're the only person in the city who already knows what happens next!'

'In the beginning, the people inside the fort refuse to let them in but then someone inside opens the gate near Raj Ghat. The sepoys then insist on meeting the king, Bahadur Shah Zafar, and declare him the emperor of India, the *shahenshah* of Hindustan. Bahadur Shah is not really very keen, but he is bullied by the sepoys and his sons and finally gives in.'

'So the Mughal royal family joins the fight? Cool!'

'Some fight!' Mr Maj gave a disapproving snort. 'These royal men were not warriors like Babur or Akbar. They didn't know how to lead an army, and they just let the sepoys do whatever they wanted. Next, the sepoys will ride out into the city, and things will get very bad, very fast.'

'Fighting in the streets?'

Mr Maj nodded. 'More like killing. The English did not have soldiers in Delhi, and the sepoys killed all the Europeans and Indian Christians they could find . . .' He sighed. 'And when the East India Company's army captured Delhi again, they massacred Indians and forced the rest to leave the city.' He shook his head sadly. 'Abysmal cruelty on both sides, the way it always is during a war.'

By then they had reached the Raj Ghat gate, where the sepoys had already arrived and a local crowd had gathered. Clearly the arrival of the sepoys had made the royal guards very nervous. There were a lot of hot arguments as the guards tried to keep the gates closed.

The sepoys looked excited and angry, and one man yelled at the guards, 'You can't stop us! We have come to meet our badshah! We are going to end the angrez sarkar! Let us in!'

As Rohan watched, some men pushed the guards and entered the fort, followed by the others. Rohan and Mr Maj trailed them at a distance. The sepoys got off their horses and began to rush towards a marble building, yelling, 'Huzoor Badshah, *salamat*! Come out, Jahanpanah!'

Rohan and Mr Maj stood a little way off, watching, and Mr Maj said, 'That's the *khwabgah*, the personal palace of the king. Poor Bahadur Shah, he doesn't know it yet but he's in for a bad time.'

'Why? They'll make him emperor!'

'He didn't *want* to lead a rebellion. He was a gentle old man who was living peacefully on a pension from the English.'

'Poet, wasn't he?' Rohan asked vaguely.

'Wonders will never cease! You remembered that!' Mr Maj grinned at Rohan. 'Yes, he wrote under the pen name of Zafar and was quite a good poet. But he was no warrior and did not have the ability to rule a kingdom. In fact, all the Mughals after Aurangzeb were pretty disastrous as rulers.'

Rohan's knowledge of history seemed to have been revived magically. 'He was banished, wasn't he, after the uprising failed? And his sons were killed?'

'Correct! Sons, grandsons—all killed by the English . . . Soon Zafar will be banished to Rangoon in Burma and will later die there, far away from his homeland. And the Mughal dynasty will die with him.'

'We can't change anything, can we? Even though we know what will happen. Y'know, sort of warn the poor guy?'

Mr Maj gave a sad shake of his head. 'Nah! We can just watch.'

'Time-travelling is not always much fun, is it?'

'Not always.'

As they watched, the door of the palace opened and a thin, frail white-haired man came tottering out, looking both puzzled and afraid. He did not look very regal, wearing a long crumpled cotton robe, like a dressing gown—which looked quite old—and there were simple leather chappals on his feet.

'I thought kings wore silks and jewellery . . .'

'Not this one. He was quite poor and trying to manage the fort on his small pension. He had many mouths to feed.'

Bahadur Shah was immediately surrounded by the excited sepoys. Rohan and Mr Maj could see the old king shaking his head and begging them to go away, and the sepoys were getting more and more agitated. Two younger men joined the king, and Mr Maj guessed they were probably Zafar's sons. The royal princes also began arguing with their father, who now sat on a charpai, dispiritedly holding his head. The whole atmosphere was making Rohan a bit nervous.

'Mr Maj, I think we should go back now,' he whispered. 'This is getting pretty serious, and I have to catch the 3 o'clock bus to go home . . .'

Suddenly they heard someone yelling in English, 'Help! Please help!', and they turned to see an Englishman being dragged out of a room by a group of sepoys. The man's clothes were torn, he looked semi-conscious and was bleeding from a wound on his head.

'Oh God! They'll kill him!' Mr Maj exclaimed and started running towards the sepoys, shouting, 'Stop! Stop! Let him go!' Rohan followed.

In his anxiety to save the poor man, Mr Maj had clearly forgotten that he could not change past events. When he and Rohan reached the group surrounding the Englishman, the soldiers glared at them, and they were immediately surrounded by angry, suspicious men. No one was willing to listen to Mr Maj, and they watched helplessly as the injured man was dragged away.

A soldier looked at Mr Maj, his eyes full of distrust. 'Who are you? Why are you trying to stop us?'

Another man moved closer. 'Are you Christians? Is that why you are trying to save that angrez?'

'No . . . no . . .' Rohan reached out an arm to protect Mr Maj, and the soldier grabbed his wrist and growled, 'What is this? Is this a hidden weapon?' Rohan's sleeve had fallen back to reveal his watch. 'Are you spies, trying to kill us?'

'And this?' Another soldier pointed to Mr Maj's spectacles. 'Where have you come from? You must be Christians!'

And then they heard a man yell, 'Kill them!'

Mr Maj was trying to plead with the men, but Rohan knew it was time for action. He remembered his karate moves and butted one man in the stomach with sudden force, making him fall to the ground, and then, kicking another soldier in the shin, he began to run, yelling, 'Mr Maj, RUN!' And somehow the old man broke free and came stumbling behind him.

The men began to chase them, and Rohan grabbed Mr Maj's hand to pull him along. With no escape route in sight, they whipped around a corner and, struggling up a flight of steps, entered a small room. Rohan slammed the door shut and put a wooden bar across it.

He turned and said urgently, 'Quick! Recite the mantra!'

'Oh . . . oh . . .' Mr Maj was searching frantically in his kurta pockets as the door began to shake, the men outside pushing against it. 'Where did I keep it? Where is it?'

'YOU LOST IT?'

Just then, one of the door jambs broke loose with a horrible *craaack*.

'Here . . . here . . .' Mr Maj found the piece of paper and, as Rohan held on tightly to his arm, he began to recite breathlessly, 'Take a step . . .'

Just as the door broke completely and fell with a crash and the soldiers surged into the room, the old man reached the end of the poem and yelled in triumph, 'NAMAH SHIVAYAH!'

Rohan joined in with a shout. 'DELHI 2018!'

With a whirring and a buzzing, the palace walls and the sepoys began to spin faster and faster in that freaky tornado way. Then there was a thud, a thump—and silence.

Very, very carefully Rohan opened his eyes and . . . Oh, fantastic, fabulous joy! There he was standing in the school library next to the table with his notebook lying on it! Mr Maj, looking a bit dishevelled, was beside him. But Rohan noticed something rather odd about the old man—he seemed to be kind of shimmering and fading at the edges.

'Oh Lord, you're vanishing, sir!'

'Of course I am . . . .' Even his voice was getting weaker. 'This is 2018 and I'm a ghost now, you—'

'Nincompoop . . . ectoplasm . . . oaf . . . yeah, I know.' Rohan smiled, feeling a sudden flood of affection for the old man. 'But, sir, I want to travel with you again. Won't you come back, please, Mr Maj?'

'I will if you call, but remember, we'll have to start time-travelling immediately or I will start fading away like I am doing now. Just come to the library and call me. But, Rohan Trivedi, I WON'T travel with a numbskull who gets 8½ out of 20—got it?'

'I get it totally. I'll ace this classwork, sir!' Mr Maj was nearly transparent now. 'Do I need a new mantra to call you, sir?'

'You certainly do! How clever of you to guess! Now write this down.'

Rohan sat down, flipped open his notebook and grabbed a pen as Mr Maj dictated, his voice receding and growing faint, as if he were speaking from somewhere far, far away.

> Calling Sri Girish Kumar Majumdar,
> O great traveller of history.
> Listen to time's echoing radar,
> O wondrous genius of mystery.

By then his voice was close to a whisper. 'And then close your eyes and call out to me twice—"Come back, Mr Maj! Come back!"'

Writing busily, Rohan stumbled a bit over the spelling of 'wondrous', and when he looked up, he found that Mr Maj had vanished.

Looking down, he discovered that Mr Maj had left a small gift behind. Next to *An Advanced History of India*, gleaming softly in the light, lay a shining gold coin—the lovely Mughal mohur. With a happy sigh, Rohan slipped the mohur into his pocket and opened the book written by R.C. Majumdar. Another Mr Maj, it seemed.

The next day, to Miss Menon's utter astonishment, Rohan submitted such an excellent essay that she gave him 17 out of 20. She was so totally thrilled with the description of the first days of the uprising in Delhi, especially his account of the sepoys crossing the river by riding over the boat bridge, that she pinned it to the class noticeboard. And Rohan hadn't even bothered to add any quotations from the history books, not that he was going to remind her of that of course.

Historical Note

British historians like to call the Uprising of 1857 just a mutiny by soldiers, but it was much more than that. The revolt spread to every section of society, and people of every caste and religion fought side by side. However, it was limited to the regions of Delhi, Uttar Pradesh and Bihar, and the rest of India remained peaceful. After a tough fight, the British won because they had better weapons as well as trained and disciplined soldiers. Later, this uprising inspired our freedom movement as we learnt an important lesson from the events of 1857—that to defeat our colonial masters we had to be united.